THE
Enid Blyton
STORY

So long as one child tells me that my work brings him pleasure, just so long shall I go on writing.

Enid Blyton

But which will survive the verdict of the years – the latest Enid Blyton or *The Wind in the Willows*? I venture to predict that Enid Blyton's stories, although they meet a popular need, are ephemeral, for their characters are puppets.

Eileen Colwell

Be commercial. What is art, anyway? It's what people like. So give them what they like. There's nothing wrong with being commercial.

Walt Disney

THE

Enid Blyton

STORY

BOB MULLAN

Acknowledgements

A number of people have helped me with this
project, and in particular I would like to thank
the staff of Darrell Waters Ltd, who allowed me
to utilise their library, Sarah Mahaffy, Mary
Tapissier, Richard Denyer and Eileen Urwin.

The author and publishers are grateful
for permission to reproduce illustrations,
sources for which are cited in the list of
illustrations. Thanks are also due to Andre
Deutsch Ltd for quotations from *The Blyton
Phenomenon* by Sheila Ray (1982), to Hodder
and Stoughton Ltd for quotations from *Enid
Blyton* by Barbara Stoney (1974) and to Darrell
Waters Ltd for quotations from Enid Blyton's
diaries and from Enid Blyton material in their
collection.

The jacket illustration incorporates a portrait of
Enid Blyton (courtesy Darrell Waters), Noddy
and Big Ears (courtesy Macdonald Ltd) and the
cover illustration of *Five Go Down to the Sea*
(courtesy Hodder and Stoughton Ltd and Allied
Artists) by Gerry Haylock.

First published in 1987 by Boxtree Limited
Text copyright © 1987 Bob Mullan

ISBN 1 85283 201 0

Designed by Grahame Dudley

Typeset by Peter MacDonald, Twickenham

Printed in Italy

for Boxtree Limited,
25, Floral Street, London WC2E 9DS

CONTENTS

BIBLIOGRAPHY

Avery, Gillian (1975) *Childhood's Pattern: a Study of the Heroes and Heroines of Children's Fiction 1770–1950*, Hodder and Stoughton: London

Bannerman, Helen (1899) *The Story of Little Black Sambo*, Chatto and Windus: London

Bawden, Nina (1975) *The Peppermint Pig*, Victor Gollancz: London

Blishen, Edward (1977) *A Golden Age of Rubbish: Quality in Children's Fiction*, pp 7–10, in Culpan and Waite, eds (1977)

Blishen, Edward (1977a) *Who's Afraid of Enid Blyton?* pp 79–82, in Culpan and Waite, eds (1977)

Blume, Judy (1979) *It's Not the End of the World*, Pan: London

Blyton, Enid (1922)* *Child Whispers*, J. Saville: London

Blyton, Enid (1924) *The Enid Blyton Book of Fairies*, Newnes: London

Blyton, Enid (1924a) *The Zoo Book*, Newnes: London

Blyton, Enid (1935) *Hedgerow Tales*, Methuen: London

Blyton, Enid (1937) *Adventures of the Wishing Chair*, Newnes: London

Blyton, Enid (1938) *The Adventures of Binkle and Flip*, Newnes: London

Blyton, Enid (1938a) *Mr Galliano's Circus*, Newnes: London

Blyton, Enid (1938b) *The Secret Island*, Blackwell: Oxford

Blyton, Enid (1939) *The Enchanted Wood*, Newnes: London

Blyton, Enid (1939a) *Naughty Amelia Jane*, Newnes: London

Blyton, Enid (1940) *Children of Cherry Tree Farm*, Country Life: London

Blyton, Enid (1940a) *Children of Kidillin*, Newnes: London (first published under the pseudonym of Mary Pollock)

Blyton, Enid (1940b) *The Naughtiest Girl in the School*, Newnes: London

Blyton, Enid (1940c) *The Secret of Spiggy Holes*, Blackwell: Oxford

Blyton, Enid (1941) *The Adventurous Four*, Newnes: London

Blyton, Enid (1941a) *The Secret Mountain*, Blackwell: Oxford

Blyton, Enid (1941b) *The Twins at St Clare's*, Methuen: London

Blyton, Enid (1942) *The Children of Willow Farm*, Country Life: London

Blyton, Enid (1942a) *Five on a Treasure Island*, Hodder and Stoughton: London

Blyton, Enid (1942b) *The Naughtiest Girl Again*, Newnes: London

Blyton, Enid (1942c) *The O'Sullivan Twins*, Methuen: London

Blyton, Enid (1943) *The Magic Faraway Tree*, Newnes: London

Blyton, Enid (1943a) *The Mystery of the Burnt Cottage*, Methuen: London

Blyton, Enid (1943b) *The Secret of Killimooin*, Blackwell: Oxford

Blyton, Enid (1943c) *Summer Term at St Clare's*, Methuen: London

Blyton, Enid (1943d) *The Toys Come to Life*, Brockhampton: Leicester

Blyton, Enid (1944) *Five Run Away Together*, Hodder and Stoughton: London

Blyton, Enid (1944a) *The Island of Adventure*, Macmillan: London

Blyton, Enid (1944b) *The Mystery of the Disappearing Cat*, Methuen: London

Blyton, Enid (1944c) *The Second Form at St Clare's*, Methuen: London

Blyton, Enid (1944d) *The Three Golliwogs*, Newnes: London

Blyton, Enid (1945) *Enid Blyton Nature*

*For a complete list of Enid Blyton books, see Stoney (1974) pp 221–4

Readers (nos 1-20) Macmillan: London
Blyton, Enid (1945a) *The Family at Red-Roofs*, Lutterworth: London
Blyton, Enid (1945b) *Fifth Formers at St Clare's*, Methuen: London
Blyton, Enid (1945c) *Mystery of the Secret Room*, Methuen: London
Blyton, Enid (1945d) *The Naughtiest Girl is a Monitor*, Newnes: London
Blyton, Enid (1945e) *Teddy Bear's Party*, Brockhampton: Leicester
Blyton, Enid (1946) *The Castle of Adventure*, Macmillan: London
Blyton, Enid (1946a) *First Term at Malory Towers*, Methuen: London
Blyton, Enid (1946b) *The Folk of the Faraway Tree*, Newnes: London
Blyton, Enid (1946c) *Mystery of the Spiteful Letters*, Methuen: London
Blyton, Enid (1946d) *Tales of Green Hedges*, National Magazine Company: London
Blyton, Enid (1947) *The Adventurous Four Again*, Newnes: London
Blyton, Enid (1947a) *Enid Blyton's Treasury*, Evans: London
Blyton, Enid (1947b) *Five on Kirrin Island Again*, Hodder and Stoughton: London
Blyton, Enid (1947c) *The Second Form at Malory Towers*, Methuen: London
Blyton, Enid (1947d) *The Valley of Adventure*, Macmillan: London
Blyton, Enid (1948) *The Sea of Adventure*, Macmillan: London
Blyton, Enid (1948a) *Six Cousins at Mistletoe Farm*, Evans: London
Blyton, Enid (1948b) *Third Year at Malory Towers*, Methuen: London
Blyton, Enid (1949) *Five Get into Trouble*, Hodder and Stoughton: London
Blyton, Enid (1949a) *Little Noddy Goes to Toyland*, Sampson Low: London
Blyton, Enid (1949b) *The Mountain of Adventure*, Macmillan: London
Blyton, Enid (1949c) *The Rockingdown Mystery*, Collins: London
Blyton, Enid (1949d) *The Secret Seven*, Brockhampton, Leicester
Blyton, Enid (1949e) *A Story Party at Green Hedges*, Hodder and Stoughton: London (includes the 'Little Black Doll')
Blyton, Enid (1949f) *The Upper Fourth at Malory Towers*, Methuen: London
Blyton, Enid (1950) *Five Fall into Adventure*, Hodder and Stoughton: London
Blyton, Enid (1950a) *Hurrah for Little Noddy*, Sampson Low: London
Blyton, Enid (1950b) *In the Fifth at Malory Towers*, Methuen: London
Blyton, Enid (1950c) *Secret Seven Adventure*, Brockhampton: Leicester
Blyton, Enid (1950d) *The Ship of Adventure*, Macmillan: London
Blyton, Enid (1950e) *Six Cousins Again*, Evans: London
Blyton, Enid (1950f) *The Wishing Chair Again*, Newnes: London
Blyton, Enid (1951) *The Big Noddy Book*, Sampson Low: London
Blyton, Enid (1951a) *Five on a Hike Together*, Hodder and Stoughton: London
Blyton, Enid (1951b) *Here Comes Noddy Again*, Sampson Low: London
Blyton, Enid (1951c) *Last Term at Malory Towers*, Methuen: London
Blyton, Enid (1951d) *The Six Bad Boys*, Lutterworth: London
Blyton, Enid (1951e) *A Tale of Little Noddy*, Sampson Low: London
Blyton, Enid (1951f) *Up the Faraway Tree*, Newnes: London
Blyton, Enid (1951g) *Well Done, Secret Seven*, Brockhampton: Leicester
Blyton, Enid (1952) *The Circus of Adventure*, Macmillan: London
Blyton, Enid (1952a) *Enid Blyton Tiny Strip Books*, Sampson Low: London
Blyton, Enid (1952b) *The Mystery of the Strange Bundle*, Methuen: London
Blyton, Enid (1952c) *Noddy and Big Ears*, Sampson Low: London
Blyton, Enid (1952d) *Secret Seven on the Trail*, Brockhampton: Leicester

Blyton, Enid (1952e) *The Story of My Life*, Pitkin: London

Blyton, Enid (1952f) *The Two Sillies and Other Stories Retold by Enid Blyton*, J. Coker: London

Blyton, Enid (1952g) *Well Done, Noddy*, Sampson Low: London

Blyton, Enid (1953) *Five Go Down to the Sea*, Hodder and Stoughton: London

Blyton, Enid (1953a) *Go Ahead Secret Seven*, Brockhampton: Leicester

Blyton, Enid (1953b) *The Mystery of Holly Lane*, Methuen: London

Blyton, Enid (1953c) *The New Big Noddy Book*, Sampson Low: London

Blyton, Enid (1953d) *Noddy is Very Silly*, Sampson Low: London

Blyton, Enid (1953e) *The Secret of Moon Castle*, Blackwell: Oxford

Blyton, Enid (1954) *The Adventure of the Secret Necklace*, Lutterworth: London

Blyton, Enid (1954a) *The Children at Green Meadows*, Lutterworth: London

Blyton, Enid (1954b) *Five Go to Mystery Moor*, Hodder and Stoughton: London

Blyton, Enid (1954c) *Good Work, Secret Seven*, Brockhampton: Leicester

Blyton, Enid (1954d) *Noddy and the Magic Rubber*, Sampson Low: London

Blyton, Enid (1955) *Bobs*, Collins: London

Blyton, Enid (1955a) *Noddy in Toyland*, Sampson Low: London

Blyton, Enid (1955b) *The River of Adventure*, Macmillan: London

Blyton, Enid (1955c) *Secret Seven Win Through*, Brockhampton: Leicester

Blyton, Enid (1956) *Be Brave, Little Noddy!*, Sampson Low: London

Blyton, Enid (1956a) *Five on a Secret Trail*, Hodder and Stoughton: London

Blyton, Enid (1956b) *Rat-a-tat Mystery*, Collins: London

Blyton, Enid (1957) *Secret Seven Mystery*, Brockhampton: Leicester

Blyton, Enid (1960) *Good Old Secret Seven*, Brockhampton: Leicester

Blyton, Enid (1961) *Mystery of Banshee Towers*, Methuen: London

Blyton, Enid (1962) *Five Have a Mystery to Solve*, Hodder and Stoughton: London

Blyton, Enid (1962a) *The Four Cousins*, Lutterworth: London

Blyton, Enid (1962b) *Look Out Secret Seven*, Brockhampton: Leicester

Blyton, Enid (1963) *Five are Together Again*, Hodder and Stoughton: London

Butler, Dorothy (1980) *Babies Need Books*, Bodley Head: London

Cadogan, Mary and Craig, Patricia (1976) *You're a Brick, Angela!*, Victor Gollancz: London

Carpenter, Humphrey and Prichard, Mari (1984) *The Oxford Companion to Children's Literature*, Oxford University Press: Oxford

Chambers, Aidan (1985) *Booktalk*, Bodley Head: London

Coopers, Susan (1968) *Over Sea, Under Stone*, Puffin: Harmondsworth

Cormier, Robert (1975) *The Chocolate War*, Victor Gollancz: London

Culpan, Norman and Waite, Clifford, eds (1977) *Variety is King*, School Library Association: Oxford

Darton, F.J. Harvey (1960, orig. 1932) *Children's Books in England: Five Centuries of Social Life*, Cambridge University Press: Cambridge

Dixon, Bob (1977) *Catching Them Young 1: Sex, Race and Class in Children's Fiction*, Pluto Press: London

Dixon, Bob (1977a) *Catching Them Young 2: Political Ideas in Children's Fiction*, Pluto Press: London

Egoff, Sheila, Stubbs, G.T. and Ashley, L.F., eds (1980) *Only Connect: Readings on Children's Literature*, Oxford University Press: Toronto

Elkin, Judith and Triggs, Pat (1985) *Children's Books for a Multi-Cultural Society*, Books for Keeps: London

Eyre, Frank (1971, orig. 1952) *British Children's Books in the Twentieth Century*,

Longman: London

Fisher, Margery (1964) *Intent upon Reading: a Critical Appraisal of Modern Fiction for Children*, Brockhampton Press: Leicester

Fisher, Margery (1975) *Who's Who in Children's Books*, Weidenfeld and Nicolson: London

Fry, Donald (1985) *Children Talk About Books*, Open University Press: Milton Keynes

Greene, Graham (1980, orig. 1933) 'Beatrix Potter', pp 258–65, in Egoff, Stubbs and Ashley, eds (1980)

Grenfell, Joyce (1984) *Turn Back the Clock*, Futura: London

Hildick, Wallace (1970) *Children and Fiction*, Evans Brothers: London

Hill, Janet (1977) 'A Minority View', pp 309–13, in Meek, Warlow and Barton, eds (1977)

HMSO (1982) *Language Performance in Schools: Primary Survey Report No. 2*, HMSO: London

Holbrook, David (1961) *English for Maturity*, Cambridge University Press: Cambridge

Inglis, Fred (1981) *The Promise of Happiness*, Cambridge University Press: Cambridge

Johns, W.E. (1954) *Biggles, Pioneer Air Fighter*, Thames: London (orig. published in 1932 as *The Camels are Coming*, Hamilton: London)

Kästner, Erich (1985, orig. 1929) *Emil and the Detectives*, Puffin: London

Kirkpatrick, D.L., ed (1978) *Twentieth-Century Children's Writers*, Macmillan: London

Leeson, Robert (1985) *Reading and Righting*, Collins: London

Lewis, C. Day (1961, orig. 1948) *The Otterbury Incident*, London

Lewis, C.S. (1980, orig. 1952) 'On Three Ways of Writing for Children', pp 207–20, in Egoff, Stubbs and Ashley, eds (1980)

Lewis, Jeremy (1982) 'The Mugging of Noddy', *Spectator*, August 14

Lively, Penelope (1973) *Astercote*, Piccolo: London

Martin, Constance (1970) 'South Sea Bubble', *Books*, 2, pp 26–7

McKellar, Peter (1977, orig. 1957) 'Enid Blyton', pp 222–5, in Meek, Warlow and Barton, eds (1977)

Meek, Margaret, Warlow, Aidan and Barton, Griselda, eds (1977) *The Cob Web: the Pattern of Children's Reading*, Bodley Head: London

Mortimer, Penelope (1980) 'Thoughts Concerning Children's Books', pp 101–5, in Egoff, Stubbs and Ashley, eds (1980)

Moss, Elaine (1986) *Part of the Pattern: a Personal Journey through the World of Children's Books 1960–1985*, Bodley Head: London

Ray, Sheila G. (1978) 'Enid Blyton', pp 152–4, in Kirkpatrick, ed (1978)

Ray, Sheila G. (1982) *The Blyton Phenomenon*, Andre Deutsch: London

Stoney, Barbara (1974) *Enid Blyton*, Hodder and Stoughton: London

Storr, Anthony (1980) 'The Child and the Book', pp 95–100, in Egoff, Stubbs and Ashley, eds (1980)

Thody, Philip (1982) 'Blyted Youth', *Yorkshire Post*, July 29

Townsend, John Rowe (1974, orig. 1965) *Written for Children*, Kestrel Books: London

Tucker, Nicholas, ed (1976) *Suitable for Children? Controversies in Children's Literature*, Sussex University Press: Brighton

Tucker, Nicholas (1976a) 'Introduction', pp 15–28, in Tucker, ed (1976)

Tucker, Nicholas (1977) 'The Blyton Enigma', pp 72–8, in Culpan and Waite, eds (1977)

Tucker, Nicholas (1981) *The Child and the Book: a Psychological and Literary Exploration*, Cambridge University Press: Cambridge

UNESCO (1984) *Statistical Yearbook*, UNESCO: Paris

Welch, Colin (1958) 'Dear Little Noddy', *Encounter*, vol. X(1), pp 18–23

Whitehead, Frank, Capley, A.C., Maddren, Wendy and Wellings, Alan (1977) *Children and their Books*, Schools Council Research Studies/Macmillan: London

LIST OF ILLUSTRATIONS

List of Illustrations

CHAPTER
— 1 —
ENID BLYTON

Enid Blyton (1897-1968) was the most commercially successful British children's writer of the twentieth century. With over 700 titles and about 500 million sales she easily outstrips all rivals. The Noddy books alone have sold well over 60 million copies. If Enid Blyton were alive today she would be in her eighties and, writing at her most leisurely pace, she would have passed the thousand-title barrier in about 1983. In terms of translations she is currently eighth in the all-time greats, translated into at least 126 other languages, and outdone only by the likes of Lenin, Marx, Tolstoy, Agatha Christie and Walt Disney productions. She is way ahead of her nearest competitors, with Mark Twain, Hans Christian Andersen, Charles Dickens and Robert Louis Stevenson the nearest.

However, despite Enid Blyton's obvious popularity, never in the history of children's literature has a writer provoked so many strongly held and violently expressed opinions. Her books have aroused hostility, anxiety and moral superiority among parents, teachers, educationalists and the higher-brow writers on the subject of children's literature. She has been attacked for the banality and repetitiveness of her plots, her lack of imagination, the meagreness of her vocabulary, and for her alleged racism, sexism and an over-emphasis on middle-class values.

All criticisms of her work can be summarised in the following manner. Her books are of poor literary quality ('slow poison' according to Margery Fisher), lead to an unrewarding addiction, and may make it impossible for the child to move on to 'quality' literature. Moreover, the critics argue, her books pollute the cultural air we breathe with their middle-class values, their sexism and their racism. Generations of children, on the other hand, have voted with their feet, making her the popular author that she is.

'The Adventures of Bobs'
(1926, *Sunny Stories for Little Folks*, Newnes)

Philip Thody, writing in 1982, remarked that, normally, you are neither as prolific nor as successful as Enid Blyton unless you have something slightly wrong with you. Lewis Carroll, for example, led a curious double life as the rather stuffy mathematics don Charles Dodgson and the eccentric poet who refused, in his sexual and imaginative life, to cease being a child. A.A.

Milne, although a competent minor *litterateur*, was so strangled by the success of *Winnie the Pooh* that he was unable to write anything else. The creator of Billy Bunter, Frank Richards, who wrote more than 60 million words, 'never married, was a compulsive gambler, and was so obsessed with being only 5ft 5in tall that he never went out except at night'. Enid Blyton in contrast, suggests Thody, 'seems to have been depressingly normal'.

The chubby dimpled face of infants drawn by Mabel Lucie Attwell (1879-1964), a contemporary of Enid Blyton's (1921 illustration in J.M. Barrie's *The Nursery Peter Pan* (1961), Hodder and Stoughton)

CHILDHOOD

Enid Blyton who, in her autobiography (1952), commented that she 'could write a whole book at one sitting if only I didn't have to eat or sleep', was born on 11 August 1897 at 354 Lordship Lane, East Dulwich, South London, a small apartment above a shop. 1897 saw also the births of Anthony Eden, Aneurin Bevan and Thornton Wilder, the death of Johannes Brahms, Queen Victoria's celebration of her Diamond Jubilee, the publication of H.G. Wells's *The Invisible Man*, Havelock Ellis's *Studies in the Psychology of Sex*, Sidney and Beatrice Webb's *Industrial Democracy* and the founding of the Royal Automobile Club.

Her father, Thomas Carey Blyton, was a cutlery salesman with interests in astronomy, French, German, music, painting, photography, singing, reading and writing and poetry. Thomas, originally a Sheffield man, moved from London to Beckenham, Kent, when Enid was a few months old; Enid gained two brothers while there. Barbara Stoney notes how Thomas 'delighted in his young daughter, so like himself both in appearance and temperament', with the same dark hair, 'alert brown eyes and sensitive, highly-strung nature, intent upon seeking out and enjoying life to the full'. Stoney suggests that almost from the beginning Thomas felt there was a special bond between him and Enid, and was often to tell her of the occasion on which he was convinced he had saved her life.

> She was barely three months old at the time and dangerously ill with whooping cough. The doctor, when called on that cold November evening, had looked grave and, shaking his head sadly, had told Thomas and Theresa that he doubted if their baby girl would survive until the morning, but Thomas refused to accept the doctor's opinion. He took the sick infant from his wife's arms, and all through that long winter night sat cradling her to him, keeping out the cold and willing her to stay alive. In the early hours when the crisis had passed and he had finally been persuaded to

THE FIRST CROCUS
(February)

Enid Blyton also turned her
hand to songwriting
(*Happy Year Song Book*,
undated, J. Cramer)

go to bed he had lain awake for some time, exhilarated
by the thought that he had undoubtedly saved his
daughter's life.

Clearly father and daughter spent a great deal of time in each
other's company with Thomas telling Enid all sorts of stories
based on his own life or otherwise; they would often walk
together in the countryside. Certainly in her autobiography there
are numerous positive references to her father, his love and
knowledge of animals and flowers, and their relationship. For
example Enid desperately wanted to sow some seeds, so her
father made a bargain with her. 'If you want anything badly, you
have to work for it', he said. 'I will give you enough money to
buy your own seeds, if you earn it. I want my bicycle cleaned —
cleaned *well* too.' Enid adds, 'How I worked! I kept thinking of
candy-tuft and Shirley poppies and mignonette as I rubbed up
that bicycle, and I thought of clarkia and nasturtiums and vir-
ginia stock as I pulled up handfuls of weeds.'

Enid learned to play the piano and read voraciously, including
Arthur Mee's encyclopaedias from cover to cover. She read *Alice
in Wonderland*, *Alice Through The Looking-Glass*, *The Water Babies*
('and skipped the part where all those long and extraordinary
words come'), *Black Beauty*, 'which I loved, though some of it was
too sad', and, of course, *Little Women* 'which I read again and
again.'

> Those children were real children. I am sure you like
> that book too. 'When I grow up I will write books about
> real children,' I thought. 'That's the kind of book I like
> the best. That's the kind of book I would know how to
> write.' ENID BLYTON (1952) *The Story of My Life*

In 1907 the family moved to another house in Beckenham, and
Enid enrolled at St Christopher's School for Girls in Beckenham.
However the 'family' was soon to be torn asunder in the new
home. There was increasing tension developing between Enid's
father Thomas and his wife Theresa, and this soon developed
into heated arguments. One night Stoney notes, 'Enid could not
bring herself to believe what she heard; that her mother and
father could behave to each other in this way was bad enough,
but that her beloved father could ever consider bestowing his
love on anyone outside the family — let alone another woman —
was something she found impossible to accept.' It was at this
time that Enid found both escape and solace from the distress she
felt in her 'little stories' which at bedtime she would develop in
her mind. As Stoney puts it, these 'fantasies increasingly became

Enid's father
(Source: Barbara Stoney)

her escape from the harsh reality of the violent scenes enacted downstairs, for in the happy, carefree stories she wove, there was no room for the angry voices or the slam of the front door which invariably seemed to terminate the quarrels'.

Her unconscious fears surfaced all too painfully when, shortly before her thirteenth birthday, Thomas left the house after another marital row, and the children were told of his departure by their mother. Superficial calm returned to the household with Thomas's departure, but the effect of this on Enid, who felt rejected in favour of someone else, was incalculable. Indeed Stoney interestingly observes that in 1928 (some fourteen years later) when Enid consulted a gynaecologist about her apparent infertility, she was diagnosed as having an unusually undeveloped uterus, almost that of a young girl of twelve or thirteen. And as Stoney adds, 'coincidental, perhaps but this diagnosis does seem to indicate once again the far-reaching effects upon the thirteen-year-old Enid of the departure from home of her father all those years before.'

With the hindsight of modern psychology, Enid and her

17

again that morning. The grass was quite wet, and puddles lay at the sides of the road, shining in the sun.

Fanny panted and puffed as she pushed her dolls' pram up a little hill. "Goodness me—it's hotter than ever—steamy hot! You dolls don't need any covers on you at all!"

Fanny went over the top of the hill and down towards the fields. She liked the fields, because here and there were little green ponds, and it was fun to go and watch the beetles in them, and the tiny fish.

As she went, she saw something on the path in front of her. It was a small frog. She wheeled her

2

pram carefully round it so that she wouldn't hurt it.

Then she saw another—and yet another! Good gracious, there were dozens! There they were, all hopping along, looking very busy indeed!

"Wherever have you come from, frogs?" asked Fanny, looking down at them. "All hopping

Enid Blyton's *Nature Readers*–'guidance, knowledge *and* entertainment' (*Nature Readers*, 35, pp 2–3 (1955) Macmillan)

brothers were further damaged when instructed by their mother to tell friends that their father was 'away on a visit'. Enid maintained this story exceedingly well; not even her best friends knew the truth of the matter. Once again this period of her life was marked by a slow but certain withdrawal from the family and into the safe and protective world of her stories.

As a schoolgirl Enid excelled at most subjects, and was also energetic and agile in sports. She was also a lover of practical jokes — an enthusiasm which did not wane when an adult. Out of school hours Enid also edited a schoolgirls' magazine, *Dab*, in which she wrote stories. She received the encouragement she (and any other writer) needed when at the age of fourteen she entered Arthur Mee's children's poetry competition and 'was thrilled to get a letter from the writer himself, telling her that he intended to print her verses and would like to see more of her work'. As Barbara Stoney adds, 'this encouraged her to branch out further with her writings and to send a selection of stories, articles and poems to other periodicals'.

Perhaps, as Freud would have said, it was almost inevitable that unconsciously Enid would blame her mother for her father's departure. In any event, as time went on, Enid's relationship with her mother deteriorated. In 1916 she felt she needed a break from what she saw as a claustrophobic home and, as a result of a suggestion from her confidante Mabel Attenborough (her best friend's aunt), she spent a holiday at a Suffolk farm. It was here, and in particular during visits to a Sunday School, that Enid realised what she should do with her life. Raised in the belief that she would eventually become a musician, she realised rather that she should become a teacher. Such an occupation would enable her to carry on writing and, indeed, supply her with a source of information about children's behaviour and also a knowledge of what they might like to read.

Enid immediately informed her father (not her mother, of course) that she would go to Ipswich High School, rather than music school, to train as a kindergarten teacher. Thomas, now resident in London, reluctantly agreed. Enid's move to Ipswich also meant, more profoundly, a move away from the family. Indeed it represented a final severing of family ties. As in the earlier case of her father's departure, Enid's decision to remove herself from the family required an unusual explanation in such a puritan and suburban culture. Barbara Stoney writes of Enid's mother's 'strange explanation of Enid's departure to enquiring relations and friends':

> She informed them that her daughter had left home, against her wishes, to join the Women's Land Army and that when Enid found — as she had been warned — that the life was too harsh for her, she had been 'too frightened to return home and admit her mistake.'

The Adventures of Binkle and Flip, Enid Blyton (1938)

19

Enid as a teacher
(Source: Barbara Stoney)

At the age of nineteen, Enid was never again to live with her mother and brothers. Any further contact with them virtually ceased.

In 1919, at the age of twenty-one, she qualified as a teacher and began teaching at Bickley Park School, Bickley. Her stay at the school was successful but short-lived, as in January 1920 she moved to Surbiton, Surrey, as nurse's governess to four children of the Thompson family, relations of Mabel Attenborough. Enid was to spend four happy years with the family and in that time began a small school in the house for the Thompson children and others, whose parents had heard of Enid's abilities.

There was, however, one event which intruded upon the relative tranquility of Enid's Surbiton life. Thomas, her father, had died unexpectedly and suddenly of a heart attack at the age of fifty, while fishing on the Thames at Sunbury. Most surprisingly Enid did not attend the Beckenham funeral. Of couse she may have been anxious not to meet 'the other woman', or indeed her mother, but none the less her absence from her beloved father's funeral seems almost astonishing. Or does it? Attendance at Thomas's funeral would have been facing a reality she perhaps could not bear. Possibly by not going she could keep him alive in her mind more easily. Certainly this could have been Enid's most central and profound *sublimation*; diverting the raw and basic feelings of loss and anger into more acceptable (to her) feelings and thought. Clearly this sublimation established a pattern that was to be consistent throughout her life: when faced with unacceptable or painful realities, she would push them back into her subconscious. A life of self-control and austerity, punctuated by moments of happiness and immense creative energy, beckoned.

EARLY WRITINGS

In 1921 the aspiring young writer won a *Saturday Westminster Review* writing competition, and in the next year or so wrote numerous short pieces, many commissioned. More firmly than ever she realised that it was writing for children that she enjoyed the most, and she used her lessons both to teach the children and to learn what they favoured in stories and poems. Not surprisingly she discovered that boys responded to tales of courage and bravery while the girls preferred fairy stories. Both, however, enjoyed stories of adventure and animal tales. But it was, as Barbara Stoney rightly notes, a small 'twenty-four page book of verse, published by J. Saville and Company in the summer of 1922...that first brought Enid's name before the general public'. In the preface to this book of verse, *Child Whispers*, the author demonstrates a pragmatism, indeed a business-like approach, which was to serve her well for the rest of her life.

> As I found a lack of suitable poems of the types I wanted, I began to write them myself for the children under my supervision, taking, in many cases, the ideas, humorous or whimsical, of the children themselves, as the theme of the poems. Finding them to be successful, I continued, until the suggestion was made to me that many children, other than those in my own school, might enjoy hearing and learning the poems. Accordingly this collection of verses is put forward in the hope that it will be a source of sincere enjoyment to the little people of the world.

Apparently the book was well received and, significantly, some reviewers saw in the book the language of a child: understanding and empathy were present. It has to be said, however, that Blyton's verse is at best childlike, at worst, sadly innocuous.

THE MAGIC
SNOW-BIRD
SUNNY STORIES FOR LITTLE FOLKS №86

2D.

EDITED BY ENID BLYTON

ENID BLYTON

Brer Rabbit
(*Enid Blyton's Little Books*)
(1942) pp 2–3, Evans)

Brer Rabbit rushing down the stairs.

OH, BRER RABBIT!

ONCE upon a time all the animals built themselves a pleasant house and said they would live in it happily together. But Brer Rabbit, who noticed that Brer Fox had taken the room next to his, wasn't too pleased about it. He had a sort of feeling that Brer Fox might make a mistake about bedrooms one night.

So he thought up a plan, and grinned to himself. He went out and bought a mighty fine whip with a long, curling lash. He hid this in his bedroom and didn't show it to anyone.

Now the next night all the animals were going to a party, and off they set, dressed in their best. They carefully turned out all the

DISAPPOINTMENT

Once I found a fairy
In my cup of tea.
She was nearly drowned
And wet as wet could be.

I picked her out and dried her
And asked her if she'd stay;
'Oh, no,' she said, '*I mustn't*,'
And off she flew away.

GOBLINS

When I am cross as I can be, and nothing's ever right,
Then Mummy says there's naughty goblins, hiding out of sight,
Who try to make me do what's wrong, and try to make me bad,
They like me to forget things, and make other people sad...

LOVELY FROCKS

Sunny Stories for Little Folks,
'The Magic Snow-Bird'
(1926)

In my Mummy's wardrobe, there are lots of lovely frocks,
I know because I've seen them hanging there;
There's purple, and there's orange, and a frilly one of blue,
And a yellow that is shiny like her hair...

23

Hugh and Enid
(Source: Barbara Stoney)

Incidentally, Enid's own mother, Theresa, had raven hair, so presumably the 'Mummy' so prevalent in the book of verse was quite unconnected, with Theresa perhaps remaining in Enid's mental reservoir. A second collection of poems, *Real Fairies*, was published in 1923 and indeed by the end of the year a total of 121 other items of Enid's were published — stories, verses, book reviews and short plays.

Her relentless creative energy left little time for this 26-year-old teacher to develop any new personal attachments. Perhaps personal attachments would resurrect the memories of her father and therefore make her life unbearable. However all of this was to change in 1924 when she met Major Hugh Alexander Pollock, who had joined the book publishers Newnes after a short post-war service with the Indian Army. Enid met the Major through submitting stories to the publishers and it seems, according to Barbara Stoney, to have been at first sight a most appropriate and complementary relationship.

> With his glamorous background, air of quiet authority and sophisticated manner he charmed the twenty-six-year-old, emotionally very immature Enid from the start.

MARRIAGE

Within months the Major had divorced his current wife (who had left him for someone else during the war) and re-married Enid on 28 August 1924 at Bromley Register Office. This presumably happy event went unrecorded in her diary. None of Enid's relations was invited to the wedding.

Enid's marital home was in Chelsea, a top-floor apartment between the Embankment and the King's Road. Marriage did not seem to interfere unduly with her writing career; articles, poems, stories and other such items poured from her pen. In 1925 the *Enid Blyton Book of Bunnies* was published by Newnes (re-issued in 1938 under the new title, *The Adventures of Binkle and Flip*). Binkle and Flip were two 'very naughty bunnies'.

" Hallo, Toys! You look very miserable!" said the brownies.

16

Naughty Amelia Jane
(1939)

> Binkle has got into trouble so often that he was beginning to be rather tired ot it. He was seriously thinking of turning over a new leaf and trying to be good for a change. But he very much wondered what Flip would say.
>
> He decided to tell him that night as they were getting ready for bed.
>
> 'Flip,' he said solemnly, 'what about being good for the rest of our lives?'
>
> Flip brushed the hair on his big ears and sniffed scornfully.
>
> 'Don't try to be funny,' he said.
>
> 'But I mean it,' said Binkle, rather cross with Flip's sniff.
>
> Flip stopped brushing and stared at Binkle in surprise.
>
> 'But you *couldn't* be good, Binkle,' he said at last.
>
> 'I jolly well could, then!' cried Binkle indignantly.
>
> 'I tell you I'm tired of being naughty, and playing tricks on people. I'd like to go and visit poor old Mowdie Mole, who's got a cold; and I'd like to take Dilly some of our flowers; and —'
>
> 'And go and dig up al Herbert Hedgehog's garden for him, and wash up Wily Weasel's breakfast things?' suggested Flip, giggling.
>
> 'Oh well, if you're going to be *funny*,' said Binkle, offended, 'I won't say any more. But you just wait till to-morrow morning.'
>
> Flip thought he would. He couldn't understand Binkle's fit of goodness, and he wondered if he had eaten too many carrot-tops at supper. He rather hoped Binkle *would* still feel the same in the morning, because Flip, too, was getting rather tired of being naughty. He was really a harmless little bunny, who much preferred the quietness of being good to the excitement of being naughty.

"FLIP," SAID BINKLE SOLEMNLY, "WHAT ABOUT BEING GOOD FOR THE REST OF OUR LIVES?"

Enid also devotes a poem to the two 'bad bunnies' who live in Heather Cottage, and she decides they're the 'biggest rascals ever met, since Brer Rabbit died!'

In 1926 Enid and Hugh moved from Chelsea to their first 'real home' as she put it, Elfin Cottage, a newly-built detached house in Beckenham. Not a natural 'housewife' herself, Enid gained more pleasure from her first 'real garden'. The garden, like most things in her life, provided information for her weekly column in *Teachers' World* and the other journals she wrote for. Animal life at the 'Cottage' was also written up in numerous articles. All her

THE TEACHERS WORLD, *January 5, 1923.*

Teachers' World, 5 January 1923

JANUARY.

OH, cold is the country this winterly day,
    As I hurry home after school,
The sky is a dreary and yellowish-grey,
    And ice is thick-spread on the pool.

*   *   *   *

The sparrows have ruffled their feathers up well,
    But still they are hungry and cold ;
They quarrel up there in the eaves, as they tell
    Of the long-ago June days of gold.

*   *   *   *

The owl in the barn cannot keep himself warm,
    And hides in the roof out of sight ;
There he sits huddled, a shadowy form,
    And silently waits for the night.

The rabbits are scampering over the snow,
    And leave little prints of their feet ;
They watch me with bright, hungry eyes as I go,
    And they're longing for something to eat.

*   *   *   *

But see, the sun peeps from the grey, wintry sky,
    And makes the snow gleam on the ground,
The cold little sparrows dart off for a fly,
    And chirrup that Spring is around !

*   *   *   *

The rabbits sit up on their little back-paws,
    And sniff at the sunshiny air,
The melting snow slips from the hips and the haws,
    And the sparrows flock hungrily there.

*   *   *   *

Oh, cold is the country this winterly day,
    As I hurry home after school,
But now the sun's driven the grey clouds away,
    And I hear the ice crack on the pool !

ENID BLYTON.

life Enid had been interested in animals; as she writes in her autobiography,

> All children like pets, especially, of course, dogs and cats, and even better than those they like puppies and kittens. I only had one pet as a child, and that was a kitten who was sent away after I had had it for a fortnight. I was heartbroken. I called it Chippy, I don't

know why, and I used to rush home from school to play with it.

Enid adds that when she grew up she 'certainly made up for not being allowed to have pets when I was a child!' She talks about a friendly jackdaw and magpie, Jackie and Maggie — 'they were a queer pair', and her pet toad, Terence: 'He really was a giant. He was perfectly tame, and appeared out of nowhere one rainy afternoon, climbing up on my doorstep. I couldn't *think* what was scrabbling out there — so I opened the door to look. And it was Terence!' It was, however, the purchase of 'Bobs' in 1926, a black and white smooth-haired fox terrier, that heralded the role domestic pets were to have in both her life and writings.

Sunny Stories for Little Folks, 'Gulliver in the Land of Giants' (1926)

SUNNY STORIES

Enid was making her name at the time in educational circles, through her *Teachers' World* contributions, and in her three-volume *Teachers' Treasury* (1926) and six-volume *Modern Teaching* (1928). Important as such contributions undoubtedly were, the most significant development in her work came in 1926 when she began editing the children's magazine *Sunny Stories*. The magazine, as Stoney points out, grew 'considerably in popularity over the years' and was to be 'forever associated with her name'.

By 1927 she was receiving hundreds of letters a week from children and teachers all around the world. The same year also saw her purchase a typewriter, somewhat reluctantly, and learn how to use it. Life at Elfin Cottage, at this time, took on the pattern of Enid working all day at her writing, with typewriter on *knee*, assisted in the home by a young maid, and with the evenings spent with Hugh.

Her relationship with Hugh at this time, although on occasions tempestuous, clearly gave her the security and the scope she needed to try to become more *herself*; and perhaps to begin to face up to some of the realities she had conveniently left behind. As Barbara Stoney so lucidly observes, Enid was more complex than some have painted her.

> With most people she was, outwardly, what they expected her to be: the imaginative, clever young teacher; the capable, prolific writer; the nature-loving woman of simple pleasures; the dutiful wife. Hugh had seen her play all these roles but knew and loved her for the far more complex person she undoubtedly was, amd went along with her every mood. He was her 'Bun'

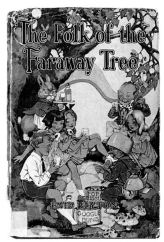

The Folk of the Faraway Tree
(1946)

and she his 'Little Bunny', nicknames Enid had given them both early in their courtship and he indulged her occasional desire to act the part of a child with a beloved father, rather than that of a wife in her early thirties. Together they built snowmen in the garden on cold winter days; played French cricket until dark on summer evenings; took part in games of 'catch' against the house wall and collected chestnuts from the tree in the front garden for 'conker' matches — '...mine is an eighter', she recorded after one contest.

On 2 August 1929 the couple moved again. Feeling threatened by the proposed building of an arterial road they moved to 'Old Thatch' in Bourne End, Buckinghamshire. By this time her popularity was increasing at an alarming rate. The Bourne End village post office organised special deliveries to Enid and 'Bobs' the dog, while Enid herself organised her readers into collecting for charity. She asked her readers if they would help to collect silver paper and foil for the Great Ormond Street Hospital to sell, and, of course, within days such materials duly arrived at Old Thatch. As Robert Leeson (1985) puts it, 'she ran blanket and silver paper collections long before *Blue Peter* was heard of'.

At Old Thatch Enid and Hugh appeared to have both a happy and more social life than ever before, yet it would be wrong to imagine that all under her roof were as happy, for Stoney documents Enid's 'rather unsympathetic conduct towards the young girls who came to work for her'. One maid was given her notice because the friend she had been out with the previous week had since developed scarlet fever. Enid, in her diaries, commented that the maid is 'now isolated in her bedroom and I have had to put off all the Whitsun parties. The girl is a fool to run straight into danger as she had done.' The maid in fact never did contract the illness, but was none the less expected to leave on the termination of the quarantine period.

October 1930 saw Hugh and Enid embark on a cruise to Madeira and the Canary Islands, aboard the *Stella Polaris*, a cruise 'remembered by her so vividly it provided her with nearly all of her foreign settings for subsequent stories' (Stoney). On return she fell 'ill' and was subsequently told she was in fact pregnant. Her diary entry was somewhat unemotional: 'he thought perhaps I was going to have a baby.' One month later, another diary entry: 'The doctor came and examined me and said for certain I am pregnant, just about three months. I am so glad. That explains the horrid sickness. Hugh and I went shopping in Maidenhead. Back to tea. Read 11pm.' As Stoney observes, 'no plans. No mention of Hugh's reaction. No hint even at any suppressed emotion.'

'He opened the door ...'
(1937, *Adventures of the Wishing Chair*, Newnes)

Page 35

He opened the door, and they all went in with the chair.

However, by Easter 1931 Enid had apparently become more excited over the impending event and even made baby clothes. And on 15 July there was the following diary entry.

Gillian was born at 6.30 this a.m. — 8¾ lbs. in weight,

122   The Folk of the Faraway Tree

the cave he was smiling. He roared with laughter as he passed the picnicking party.

"Such a joke!" he said to them. "Such a joke!"

"What was the Secret?" asked Connie.

"Ah, that's nothing to do with you!" said the brownie. "That's *my* Secret, not yours!"

The tiny goblin who had once done a wicked thing came up to the children. "Did you find out the Secret of Forgetting?" asked Bessie.

The goblin nodded.

"I'll tell it to you, because then if you do a wrong thing, maybe you can get right with yourself afterwards," he said. "It's so dreadful if you can't. Well, the Wizard Tall-Hat told me that if I can do one hundred really kind deeds to make up for the one very bad one I did, maybe I'll be able to forget a little, and think better of myself. So I'm off to do my first kind deed."

"DID YOU FIND OUT THE SECRET OF FORGETTING?" ASKED BESSIE

21½ inches in length, a lovely child. Hugh is delighted. A very easy confinement all over in five hours. Dr. Poles delivered baby and Dr. Bailey gave chloroform. I came round about 7 feeling very hungry and comfortable. Baby sucked as soon as she was put to the breast. Hugh went up to town in afternoon.

Her readership was told of the new arrival through the pages of the 26 August edition of *Teachers' World*: 'A lovely new pet has come to Old Thatch. Some of you have heard the news already, but I know a great many of you have not, because the pet arrived in the holidays. You can have three guesses — what is it? I am sure you are nearly all wrong, so I must tell you. Well, the new pet is a little baby girl!'

Within three months of Gillian's birth Enid had installed a young untrained nanny to look after Gillian day and night, for she slept in the nursery with the baby.

In 1935 'Bobs', Enid's beloved dog, fell ill and eventually died, and although she mentioned it in her diary she refused to speak of his death to anyone. Like her father Thomas, 'Bobs' still lived on. His 'letters' continued to appear for as long as she wrote her page and her readers were unaware of his death. A year or so earlier, however, Enid was forced to accept another reality, namely that through increased stress at work Hugh had sought comfort in alcohol and was becoming quite ill.

Another child, another daughter Imogen, was born to Enid on 27 October 1935 (following a miscarriage the previous year), 'a sweet little baby' Enid was to record in her diary.

The Wishing Chair flies away (1938 edition, *Adventures of the Wishing Chair*, Deans)

ADVENTURES OF THE WISHING CHAIR

In January 1937 *Sunny Stories* magazine appeared in a new format, with long serial stories; the first of these was brought out in book form as *Adventures of the Wishing Chair* at the end of the year.

As Sheila Ray (1982) notes, most 'modern fantasy stories have their roots in traditional myth, legends and folk tales'. C.S. Lewis in his *Narnia* books draws on Christian myth and Norse legend, Tolkein uses Norse and Anglo-Saxon legends, Alan Garner Norse and Welsh legends, while the 'Arthurian Story has been a source of inspiration for many recent writers such as Penelope Lively, William Mayne, and Susan Cooper'. She adds that the idea of the Wishing Chair is both simple and attractive, but does not seem to link directly to any traditional story, although Enid Blyton may have known Frances Browne's (1856) *Granny's Wonderful Chair*. Certainly there are similarities. In Brown's book a girl called Snowflower lives in a cottage with her grandmother, who goes away on a journey, leaving her chair as company for the child. Every night it tells Snowflower a story, and, when she wishes to travel, it takes her anywhere she wants to go. In Blyton's story, Mollie and Peter are trapped in an antique shop by a pixie-like man and a wizard. Worried by the events around them Peter, 'making no movement to get out of the chair, in which he and Mollie were still sitting with their legs drawn up', proclaims 'I wish we were safely at home!' Enid Blyton then takes up the story:

And then the most extraordinary thing of all happened! The chair they were in began to creak and groan, and suddenly it rose up in the air, with the two children in

it! They held tight, wondering whatever was happening! It flew to the door, but that was shut. It flew to the window, but that was shut too...The chair finding that it could not get out of the door or the window, flew up the little stair-way. It nearly got stuck in the doorway at the top, which was rather narrow, but just managed to squeeze itself through. Before the children could see what the room upstairs was like, the chair flew to the window there, which was open, and out it went into the street. It immediately rose up very high indeed, far beyond the housetops, and flew towards the children's home. How amazed they were! And how tightly they clung to the arms! It would be dreadful to fall!

'I say, Mollie, can you hear a flapping noise?' said Peter. 'Has the chair got wings anywhere?'

Mollie peeped cautiously over the edge of the chair.

'Yes!' she said. 'It has a little red wing growing out of each leg, and they make the flapping noise! How queer!'

The Magic Faraway Tree
(1986)

Green Hedges
(Source: Darrell Waters
Group)

The chair began to fly downwards. The children saw that they were just over their garden.

'Go to our playroom, chair,' said Peter quickly. The chair went to a big shed at the bottom of the garden. Inside was a playroom for the children, and here they kept all their toys and books, and could play any game they liked. The chair flew in at the open door and came to rest on the floor. The children jumped off and looked at one another.

'The first real adventure we've ever had in our lives!' said Mollie, in delight. 'Oh, Peter, to think we've got a magic chair — a wishing-chair!'

And then, not surprisingly but also quite enjoyably, Peter, Mollie and the chair have all sorts of adventures with Grabbit Gnomes, the Ho-Ho Wizard, the witch Kirri-Kirri, Big-Ears the Goblin, the Snoogle 'the funniest-looking creature they had ever seen', and many others. On a more technical point, one problem which the 'author of fantasy' has to solve is that of involving the child characters in magic without the adult characters becoming aware of this involvement. As Sheila Ray notes, it is a problem which 'would intrigue many child readers, but Enid Blyton ignores it completely'. Peter and Mollie have a 'convenient playroom, a shed at the bottom of the garden', where they can hide the chair, and they contrive to have all their adventures at times when they will not be missed.

Ray observes, quite rightly, that the creatures of fantasy —
elves, fairies, gnomes and giants — are to be found in many of
Enid Blyton's short stories where, 'apart from their magical
powers, they tend to behave in a rather human way'. This is
presumably due to the obvious fact that it is extremely difficult to
draw fantasy creatures in such a way as to make them unique,
especially when one is writing so quickly. Ray unfavourably
compares Blyton's fantasy writings with those of Hilda Lewis
(1939) in *The Ship That Flew* (also incidentally set in an antiques
shop) and Edith Nesbit's Psammead stories of the bad-tempered
magical being in, for example, *Five Children and It* (1902). Unlike
those books Enid Blyton, she argues, make very little reference to
historical figures or other literature: 'literary allusion in *The
Enchanted Wood* (1939) stretches only to Goldilocks and the Three
Bears, whom Fanny and Bessie seek out to help rescue Jo from the
Land of Ice and Snow'. On the other hand she praises Blyton for
achieving the difficult task of distinguishing the children from
each other and developing them well in *The Enchanted Wood*.
Further, although Enid Blyton's humour is mainly of the elemen-
tary slapstick variety (like her schoolgirl penchant for practical
jokes) she does, Ray adds, create some successful comic characters in the book.

"WELL, LOOK! THERE'S A COTTAGE," SAID JUMP.
(See page 21.)

Enid Blyton Book of Brownies,
1926

> Dame Washalot, who pours her dirty washing water
> away down the Tree regardless of who is coming up,
> and Mister Watzisname, who spends most of his time
> asleep and is angry if woken up, provide regular hum-
> orous hazards. The cheerful Moon-Face and fairylike
> Silkie act as guide to the magic elements. The most
> striking character, however, is undoubtedly the Sauce-
> pan Man who provides a different kind of humour; he
> is hung all over with saucepans and kettles and is
> invariably deafened by the continual clashing of the
> pots and pans.

Ray argues that the Nesbit and Lewis books have 'clear geographical settings' — *The Ship that Flew* is set firmly on the south
coast, and *Five Children and It* in Kent — whereas Enid Blyton's
books could be located almost anywhere. That, of couse, may be
to Blyton's advantage. There are similarities between the books:
in both *Five Children and It* and Blyton's *The Enchanted Wood*
'town and country are contrasted', and the country is seen as a
place where unusual things happen. However, the difference is
clear when the two houses central to each story are described.

Blyton's is a stereotyped dream cottage, described as

sweet. Roses hung from the walls — red and white and pink — and honeysuckle was all round the front door. It was lovely.' No indication is given of its location. Nesbit's 'was not really a pretty house at all, it was quite ordinary' but it is placed geologically in the first paragraph, between a chalk quarry and a gravel pit, and we later learn that it is in Kent and that Rochester is the nearest town. (Ray, 1982)

If *The Enchanted Wood* had little historical connection with other literature, the same cannot be said of *The Magic Faraway Tree* (1943), where there are striking similarities between the Faraway Tree and the Norse Tree Yggdrasil. Whereas the roots of Yggdrasil reach down into other worlds, the upper branches of the Faraway Tree lead into a succession of strange worlds. A red squirrel plays an important part in the life of the Faraway Tree, just as he does in the life of Yggdrasil: it is his job to ease travel up and down the tree.

The helpful red squirrel (1985 edition, *The Magic Faraway Tree*, Deans)

Mother did ask, of course, and the girls told her what had happened.
"I find all this very difficult to believe," said Mother, astonished. "I think Jo is just spending the night with Moon-Face for a treat. Well, he certainly must come back to-

'What do we do with the cushions?' asked Dick. 'Does Moon-Face want them back?'

'Yes, he does,' said Fanny, picking them up. 'The red squirrel always collects them and sends them back to him.' As she spoke, a red squirrel, dressed in a jersey, popped out of a hole in the trunk.

'Here are the cushions,' said Fanny, and the squirrel took them. He looked up into the tree, and a rope came swinging down.

'Moon-Face always lets it down for his cushions,' said Bessie. Dick watched the squirrel tie the three cushions to the rope end. Then he gave three gentle tugs at the rope, and at once the rope was pulled up, and the cushions went wringing up the tree to Moon-Face. (*The Magic Faraway Tree*)

Adventures unfold in lands of toys ('golliwogs, teddy bears, dolls of all kinds, stuffed animals and clockwork toys), angry pixies,

'Off the children go through the Enchanted Wood' (1985 edition, *The Magic Faraway Tree*, Deans)

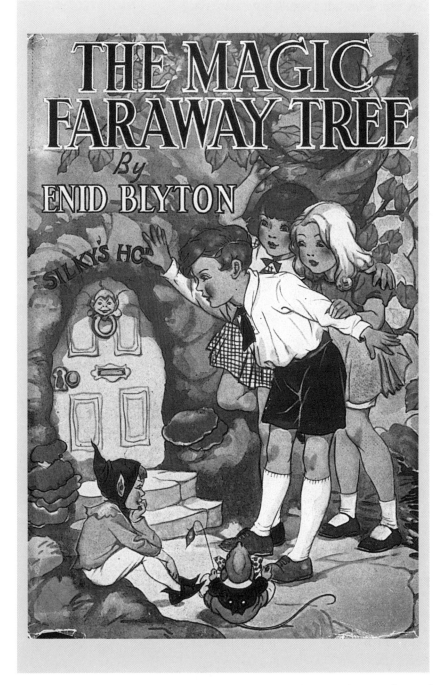

The Magic Faraway Tree
(1943)

'growing pills', adventures with friends from *The Enchanted Wood*, but in the end 'everything comes right' and they head home through the 'land of presents'.

Come on — let's go home to Mother. What a lovely adventure! I hope it won't be the last.'

It won't, because the Faraway Tree is still there. But we must leave them now to have their adventures by themselves, for there is no time to tell you any more. There they all go through the Enchanted Wood, carrying their lovely presents — what a lucky lot of children they are, to be sure!

Sheila Ray, in assessing *The Magic Faraway Tree*, points to a mixture of qualities in Blyton's writings which were repeated again and again over the years: 'with all the cruel, frightening and sad elements of the legendary Norse tree removed, and with all the difficult names omitted, one can see that this is what might be left.' But, she adds, 'surprisingly Enid Blyton's use of a tree as a gateway to fantasy worlds seems to be unique'.,

Enid's world of fantasy is not of the same stature in terms of plot, style or profundity as C.S. Lewis's *Narnia* or Frank Baum's *Oz*, but some commentators regard these stories of hers as representing much of her best work.

HUGH'S ILLNESS

In the late 1930s it became clear to Hugh that Enid was not only gaining her own fame and fortune, but additionally was becoming increasingly self-assured. As Barbara Stoney puts it, 'he was also beginning to feel that their roles in the household were being reversed and that he was fast becoming superfluous to her affairs'. To add to his worries, he was suffering stress at work, and was also convinced that soon the country would once again be at war.

> The more depressed he became over the possibility of such a catastrophe, the easier he found it to fall back on his old means of consolation. But fearing that Enid would suspect his motives and despise him the more if he drank openly, he took his bottles into a small cellar under the stairs, only accessible through the maid's bathroom, and out of sight from the rest of the house …It was, therefore, not until Hugh became seriously ill in the early summer of 1938, and some of the undisposed-of bottles were discovered, that the rest of the household became aware of what had been going on. (Barbara Stoney)

He was forgiven and life returned to normal, with the Blytons looking for a larger house for the burgeoning family and staff. A house was duly found in two-and-a-half acres of grounds in Beaconsfield, Buckinghamshire. She asked her readers to suggest a name for her new house, and from their suggestions she chose 'Green Hedges', a name to be associated with Enid from then on.

The Two Sillies
(1952)

CHAPTER
— 2 —
CIRCUSES AT HOME
AND ELSEWHERE

An interesting episode occurred in 1932, which both demon-strated Enid's determination, energy and fortitude, but also perhaps touches on one of her major problems — an inability to take her time. She began 1932 by embarking on a new project, one she had long wanted to attempt — her first full-length *adult* novel. By 5 February of the same year she had completed the book. In her diary she recorded, 'finished my novel! About 90,000 words. It's called *The Caravan Goes On.*' However she was unable to place the novel with a publisher and it was never mentioned again. Barbara Stoney conjectures that 'Enid was never one to waste anything over which she has spent time and effort,' so that

> It seems likely that the novel eventually reappeared, in a shortened form, as a children's book. The title suggests it may well have been transposed into *Mr Galliano's Circus* (1938) which contained several strong, adult characters — unlike most of Enid's other books in which children figure in the dominant roles.

Determined as ever, however, Enid 'put aside her disappoint-ment and set to work on several new commissions', but the only stories she wrote from then on were for children. Indeed *Mr Galliano's Circus* was the third long serial story she wrote for *Sunny Stories*, and destined to be the first of another well-loved series of books, based on life in a circus. Sheila Ray provides the context.

> The circus seems to have had a special attraction for Enid Blyton for the word 'circus' appears in the title of

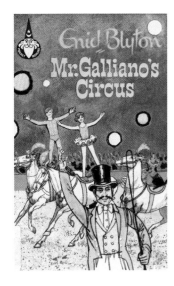

Mr Galliano's Circus
(1967)

twelve of her books and she also used visits to the circus or circus backgrounds in her other stories. For example, the girls of St Clare's go to see Galliano's Circus and Carlotta, one of the pupils at the school, comes from a circus background and is capable of doing 'marvellous tricks.' To some extent, this probably reflects the importance of the circus as a source of children's entertainment in the 1930's, when a small touring circus was still a viable economic possibility and before the audience's expectations were raised too high by television presentations. However, the circus also contained elements which were intrinsically appealing to Enid Blyton, such as the animals, the spectacular successes, the excitement, the romance and the unusual characters.

Ray points to other authors who have used circuses as backgrounds to stories and in particular mentions Howard Springs's *Sampson's Circus*, one of the 'most sophisticated' circus books, and hence one which 'has never been particularly popular with children'. *Mr Galliano's Circus* is about the 'adventures' — rescuing stray animals, curing a sick dog, teaching his own dog tricks, learning to walk the tightrope — of Jimmy Brown. Jimmy Brown, who is poor because his father is unemployed, likes animals, and would like to go the circus but cannot afford a ticket. He is however allowed to help in the circus, is befriended by Lotta the bareback rider, and when the circus carpenter disappears with the takings he manages to get the job for his father, and the Brown family join the circus. The story ends at the point at which Lotta's parents are leaving the circus to perform elsewhere, and it looks as it Lotta will have to go too, until kind Mrs Brown invites her to stay with them.

Sheila Ray unfavourably compares *Mr Galliano's Circus* with another circus book of the same period, Noel Streatfield's *The Circus Is Coming* (1938). For example, she notes that Streatfield's circus is motorised and visits 'real places', whereas Enid Blyton's is horsedrawn ('there seems to have been some confusion in her mind between gipsies and circuses since the circus caravans are described as clip-clopping down country lanes with smoke coming out of their chimneys, in a very romantic way'), that Streatfield is 'careful to set out the regulations concerning child performers' while Enid Blyton ignores the requirements of compulsory education completely and both Jimmy and Lotta perform, despite the fact that they are too young to do so, without a hint that they require special permission from the authorities. Ray concludes that 'Lotta lives out a common young female

'Jimmy meets Lotta'
(1938, *Mr Galliano's Circus*, Newnes)

14   Mr. Galliano's Circus

"COME UP THE LADDER AND HAVE A PEEP," SAID THE LITTLE GIRL.

'Jimmy performs on the elephant's back' (1938, *Mr Galliano's Circus*, Newnes)

HOW THEY STARED WHEN THEY SAW JIMMY ON THE ELEPHANT

fantasy. Dressed like a fairy from the top of the Christmas tree, she rides into the circus ring on the back of a horse and performs a succession of wonderful tricks for the admiring and applauding audience.'

Now clearly there *is* a difference between the two books. For a start the authors' methods are different, in that Enid Blyton did little if no research for her books, but rather relied on her imagination and experience, whereas Noel Streatfield, for example, for her circus book toured for several months with Bertram Mills Circus to gather material. More importantly there is the difference of realism, which Ray clearly considers to be an issue of importance. But is it? For a start, children do realise at an early age that there is a world of books and a world of reality, and that such worlds are different. If a child wanted to know more of the real world, it could look elsewhere. While if 'Lotta lives out a common young female fantasy', the author can only be congratulated for sharing and understanding such a daydream. Ray also criticises Blyton for the fact that the adult characters in her circus book are 'stereotypes and exist solely in relation to the children'. For example, she points to the fact that Mr Galliano's moods are immediately detectable from the position of his top hat — 'the further it is on the side of his head, the happier he is' — which is a fair 'indication of the level of adult characterization'. But wasn't that *precisely* Blyton's skill in attracting readers: a child's view of the world? Sheila Ray concludes that *Mr Galliano's Circus* provides a 'simple and entertaining read', one which would enable the child to progress to the more detailed books like *Sampson's Circus* and *The Circus is Coming*. Exactly. As we shall see later, Blyton's massive contribution to children's literature and children's reading skills was the ability to get the child reading in the

The Circus of Adventure
(1979)

first place. She was, presumably, not expecting to re-write Lewis Carroll's *Alice's Adventures in Wonderland* everytime she put pen or typewriter to paper.

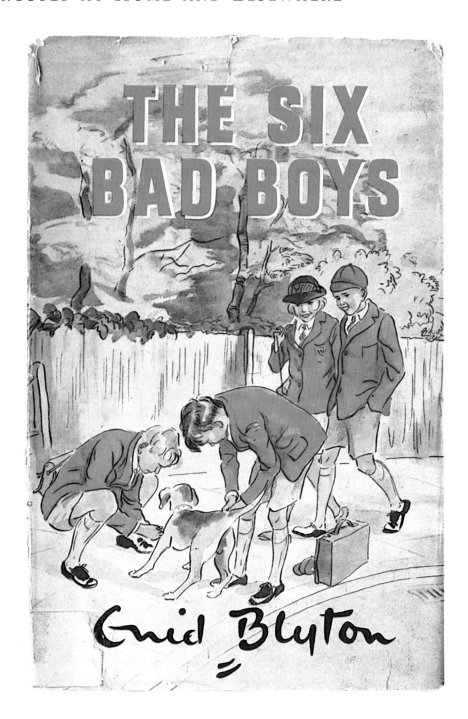

In *The Circus of Adventure* (1952) the circus is used to add an extra dimension to the adventure story: Jack, separated from some other children, falls in with a travelling circus and per-

'The Mackenzies'
(1951, *The Six Bad Boys*,
Lutterworth)

" *That boy Tom is fond of his father,*"   *said his wife, still darning at top speed.*

suades two acrobats to help him rescue the children from the Ruritarian Castle, where they are imprisoned, by means of a tightrope and trapeze swing. In the book we also see glimpses of Enid Blyton's social snobbery, or, as Bob Dixon (1977) puts it, her 'insistence on conformity – and conformity to the most narrow, establishment-type beliefs, practices and values', although this can, of course, be partly explained by her own life and circumstances, and the period in which she wrote.

> Jack liked Pedro very much. He was only a circus boy, with rough manners and ways...

while on the other hand

> The circus-folk approved of Jack. He was willing and quick, and he had good manners, which made him very popular with the women, who had got used to rough ways from the men-folk. Jack liked most of the circus people — they were kindly and generous, quick-tempered and cheerful — but they were dirty and slovenly, too, not always very honest and sometimes lazy...They were a curious lot.

FAMILY LIFE STORIES

Novels of family life in children's literature have their origin in the moral tales of the late eighteenth and early nineteenth centuries, which used the events of an ordinary home life to make instructive points about good and bad behaviour. An early and influential book was Charlotte M. Yonge's (1856) *The Daisy Chain*, a book which probably gave Louisa Alcott a model for the classic *Little Women* (1868). The first British classic family story was Edith Nesbit's (1899) *The Story of the Treasure Seekers*, while an interesting later product was Eve Garnett's (1937) *The Family From One End Street*, seen by many as one of the few genuine working-class family stories, although later regarded as somewhat patronising.

The family novel is concerned with personal relationships, mainly between brothers and sisters, children and their parents, or between the family and the local community. Alcott's *Little Women*, also known as *Meg, Jo, Beth and Amy*, described a few months in the lives of the March sisters when their father is away from home as an army chaplain in the American Civil War. The girls are befriended by Theodore Lawrence, known as 'Laurie', the grandson of a rich old gentleman next door. Incidents and dramas involve the girls, but in the end they are reunited with their father. Interestingly, especially given the time of Alcott's writing career, she showed a progressive attitude when asked to write a sequel to her successful *Little Women*: 'Girls write to ask who the little women marry, as if that was the only end and aim of a woman's life. I *won't* marry Jo to Laurie to please any one' (Carpenter and Prichard, 1984). Such progressive attitudes were not at the heart of Enid Blyton's work, as we shall see, although they were not entirely absent.

Blyton's most well-known family stories are *The Family at Red-Roofs* (1945) and *The Six Bad Boys* (1951). Sheila Ray outlines the story of *The Family at Red Roofs*.

" Finding's keeping," said Fred, his eyes gleaming.

'Finding's keeping' (1951, *The Six Bad Boys*, Lutterworth)

> The story begins with the Jacksons moving to a new house after father has been promoted, a prospect of new prosperity ahead. Father goes abroad on business, his ship is wrecked and he is apparently drowned; meanwhile Mrs Jackson is taken ill. The family survives the various disasters and the story ends happily when father returns.

This Blyton story, unusually, is marked by precise domestic detail. Constance Martin, in a 1970 review, has argued that compared with *Little Women* Blyton's is 'milk-and-water' and moreover that one of the characters, seventeen-year-old Molly, is more like a child of ten. Sheila Ray adds that Blyton's 'anxiety to point a moral seems to prevent her from allowing her characters to develop and mature through their experiences'. However Ray does add that is was partly a 'forward looking' book, in that one of the characters says 'I think every girl ought to have some kind of work to do.'

'The boys face the
magistrates'
(1951, *The Six Bad Boys*,
Lutterworth)

THE SIX BAD BOYS

The book raises a number of interesting issues, not last the fact
that many have seen it as an attempt at both social realism and as
an exercise in writing out sublimated feelings of anger and loss
when her father Thomas left some forty years earlier. Certainly
there are similarities: the three 'Berkeley' children (two girls and
a boy) are deserted by their father after numerous violent quarrels between their parents. As Barbara Stoney observes, the
'effect of his departure had on the children and the subsequent
behaviour of the mother — even to the pledging of the family to
secrecy over his disappearance — was an echo of this desperately
unhappy period of Enid's life, yet such was her reticence about
her early years no one guessed at the time that she was writing
from personal experience.'

With *The Six Bad Boys* Enid Blyton was both writing a story and
attempting to reflect the reality of the perceived social problems
of the time, at a time when British psychiatrists were becoming
increasingly concerned with the parents', especially the mothers',
relationship with their children.

In a specially written preface Blyton states that the book is
'written for the whole family', and for 'anyone who has to do
with children'. She adds that the book is written to entertain the
reader, but is written also 'to explain some of the wrong things
there are in the world, and to help to put them right'.

I love children, good or bad. I know plenty of good ones — and I have been to the Juvenile Courts and seen plenty of bad ones. One of the finest magistrates of these Courts is the well-known Mr. Basil Henriques, who deals so wisely and kindly with all the delinquent children brought before him. I have watched him at his Court dealing with these children.

In trepidation, I asked him if he would be kind enough to read through my book to see if I had made any mistakes in Court procedure.

In fact the legendary Juvenile Court Chairman provided *The Six Bad Boys* with a foreword and, unlike Enid, did not portray the young simply in terms of 'good or bad'.

It is generally admitted that the 'broken home' is one of

'A happy family'
(1951, *The Big House*, Ladybird)

Father and Peter have to wait some time for Mother and Jane. Then Peter says, "I can see them now. Here they are."

Mother has bought a new hat. "I hope you like the hat I've bought," she says.

"I like it," says Peter. "You've found a nice one."

"Yes, you've picked a nice one," says Father. "I think it's lovely. We both like it."

Mother looks happy. "A woman always likes a new hat," she says. "I haven't bought another hat this year."

"We had to wait a long time," Peter says to Jane. "It made me think you were lost."

"When are we going to see the big garden?" asks Jane. "Can we go today?"

Father says, "We have too much to do today. We'll go over in two days' time. I put that in my letter to Mr White. I want to see him before he goes away. We should have a talk before he goes. Come on now, it's five o'clock and time to go home."

Enid and her animals
(Source: Darrell Waters
Group)

the main causes of children getting into trouble. It is the unhappy children rather than the 'bad' ones who come before the courts, and it is the broken home which so often causes unhappiness in children, especially when the phrase is interpreted to include the home in which the parents quarrel in front of the children, and from which the mother goes out to work at times when she is needed by them.

He adds, however, the Blyton's description of the workings of the minds of Bob Kent and Tom Berkeley 'is, in my opinion, absolutely brilliant', as it shows *why* the broken home causes children to go wrong, and the gradual deterioration of both boys is told in a manner which I have never seen surpassed'. Clearly he could not have read the book very carefully — but his comments, of course, also reflect the prevailing attitude towards criminology at the time.

Early in the book Mr and Mrs Mackenzie discuss the children of their neighbours, the Berkeleys and Mrs Kent. On Mrs Berkeley:

'Oh, but she says things in front of the children!' said Mrs Mackenzie, indignantly. 'What would you say, Andy, I'd like to know, if I told you you were a nitwit in front of the twins and Pat? That's what she said to her husband — in front of me *and* her children!'

'It's bad for the children,' said her husband. 'But maybe she said it in fun, Jessie.'

While on the subject of Bob Kent, Mrs Mackenzie considered:

'He wants a father like *you*,' said his wife, taking up the stocking again. 'He could do with a spanking now and again. He's a nice boy, but too big for his boots, sometimes. He just wants keeping in order. Like you keep the twins in order!'

Her husband grinned, and began to fill his pipe.

'Poor Donald! He got a whacking last week, didn't he, for borrowing my bicycle without telling me, and putting it back in the shed covered with mud! But he knew he deserved it.'

'Well, you're his father, and if fathers can't keep their boys on the right road it's a poor look-out for the boys!' said his wife. 'Anyway he knew he'd earned the whacking. He won't borrow things without asking again!'

Bob Kent's mother sometimes despaired over her eleven-year-old son. 'If it wasn't for you, my boy, I could go out and get a good job', said his mother. 'And one of these days I will, if you don't do what you're told.' Bob in turn felt unloved at times, and compared his own mother unfavourably with Mrs Mackenzie: 'The twins' mother was always so kind, Bob thought. She always seemed so pleased to see them whenever they came back from school. She didn't mind hugging them back when they hugged her. He was quite sure they never seemed a bother to her. She was a *real* mother.'

To make matters worse, Bob's mother *did* get a job and he had to get used to returning to a 'silent and dark' house. He used to return home from school, wash up the breakfast things and then lay the table for tea. Then he would wait. 'He was almost beside himself with worry when he heard the key of the front door put into the lock. He rushed to greet her, all his resentment forgotten in his relief.' But it was nothing compared to the Mackenzie's household.

Enid Blyton at a fete
(Source: Darrell Waters Group)

> The whole family was there. Mr Mackenzie was sitting in his chair smoking his pipe, with Pat on his knee telling him something. Mrs Mackenzie was darning, listening to something that Jeanie was telling her. Jeanie was drawing at the same time, and near her was Donald doing his homework.
>
> The fire burnt cheerfully. The cat sat in front of it, its tail curled neatly round. Frisky suddenly bounded in and made a great fuss of everyone.

Meanwhile the Berkeley's were also having troubles, and one night after a row ('she had nagged at him as usual') Mr Berkeley left the home: 'Dad! What are you going? Don't go! I don't want you to go!' Her father said nothing, but clipped shut his big suitcase...The front door slammed. The front gate clicked shut. Quick footsteps went down the lane, and then faded away.'

Neighbours did not automatically rally round Mrs Berkeley. Mrs Mackenzie proved surprisingly unsympathetic.

> 'Andy, my husband, says you had a good man and a kind one,' she said. 'He helped willingly with the properties for the school play. I liked him too. There was nothing wrong with him that I could see, Mrs Berkeley.'
>
> 'Oh, but you don't know the dreadful things he said to me,' said Mrs Berkeley, beginning to cry.
>
> 'No, and I don't want to know them,' said Mrs Mackenzie firmly. 'There are always faults on both sides,

and your biggest fault, both of you, is that you only think of yourselves and not of the children. Poor things, going about with anxious looks, pretending their father's gone on a visit! Can't you see what you're doing to those children of yours?'...

'You're unkind,' wept Mrs Berkeley. 'I wish I hadn't come to you for advice.'

'Ah well, if it's advice you're needing I'll give it to you,' said Mrs Mackenzie. 'Now you listen to me. You write to that husband of yours and tell him you're missing him and the children are too; tell him you'll turn over a new leaf for their sake, if only he'll come back.'

'Oh, I couldn't possibly do that!' said Mrs Berkeley, horrified. 'I'm not in the wrong. He's always been the one to fail us.'

Bob Kent meanwhile found his mother's work more and more unpalatable: 'You like your job better than you like me. That's all I know!' The story proceeds with the discontented Tom and Bob, who join forces with the 'Four Terrors Gang', set up a head-quarters in the cellar of a half-ruined old terrace house, and engage in petty crime ('a life of crime', Sheila Ray mistakenly calls it), including stealing from a lost wallet. They are, of course, subsequently caught by the police. Bob's mother, Mrs Kent, then has an altercation with Mrs Mackenzie: 'You're pleased my Bob has got into trouble, aren't you? Your children are all perfect, aren't they? You're *the* perfect mother, aren't you? Oh, I know what people like you are like — going round preaching at others,

Enid, Darrell Waters, Gillian and Imogen, left
(Source: Darrell Waters Group)

Book signing in a Brompton store, 1945
(The Photo Source)

and gloating when they go wrong.' Later on in the conversation Mrs Mackenzie tells Mrs Kent that she will have to attend the police court: 'All the parents always have to be there, so that the magistrate may find out exactly how much the fathers and mothers are to blame for their children's wrongdoing.'

At the court the parents are duly blamed and punished, as are the offending children. For example, Tom is sent to a school in the country, perhaps for a whole year, 'where we hope you will be happy'. He can return home when the court is satisfied 'that there is a good and happy home for him to come back to'. The magistrate then deals with Bob, who, he decides, should be sent to foster parents: 'He had the reports about Bob's mother before him — and many a time before he had similar reports of children going wrong because their mothers had left them in order to go out to work.'

The court hears from Bob's mother that she is 'ashamed of him', and furthermore that she wants to 'sell up and go right away out of the district, I feel so ashamed. And I don't want him to come with me.' And so she does, while he goes to foster parents, who are eventually replaced by — the Mackenzies. And it all ends happily ever after.

A message to her readers (1942, *Enid Blyton's Happy Story Book*, Brockhampton)

> Bob crept into the garden and went up to the window. He looked through the crack in the curtains as he had done several times the year before. He saw Mrs Mackenzie getting tea, with Jeanie at the fire, toasting bread. He saw Donald showing his mother something he bought.
>
> Then in ran Pat and her mother ruffled her hair and kissed her. Frisky leapt about, barking as usual, telling the family he was pleased to be back. Mr Mackenzie wasn't yet home — but Bob saw his pipe-rack, his slippers and his arm-chair ready for him.
>
> 'I used to envy them because I hadn't a family too,' he thought. 'But now it's my family. I don't need to peep. I belong! Here I go walking in, to join my family!'
>
> And in he went with his parcels, smiling all over his face. He didn't need to peep through curtains any more!

There is no doubt that *The Six Bad Boys* is compelling reading, particularly as most children would be able to identify with at least one family or one child. It also touches on some features of human life which interest most children — maternal love, daring and the fear of authority. Blyton broke new ground in writing a

Enid Blyton's Magazine, no. 4
(5) 13–26 February 1957

children's story book concerned with social problems. And it must be remembered that she wrote against a backcloth of a judicial system which was mainly interested only in retribution and an extremely traditional family model. Something of what she says makes sense even today, in that 'child unhappiness' can have disastrous consequences. Some of the other implications of the book, however, are less appealing.

– the best manner in which to control children is not by understanding but rather by physical force ('a good whacking').

– that children cannot adapt *either* in a single-parent family or when their mother works ('You like your job better than you like me').

– that family life revolves around the male figure, the father ('Andy, my husband, says you had a good man and a kind one').

– that the most appropriate punishment for a petty crime is not understanding but rather the separation and taking away of children.

Many would agree with Enid Blyton even today, but clearly in *The Six Bad Boys,* although a product of her times, she both misunderstands the needs of women and the nature of crime. She paints an extremely simple picture. And it does have to be remembered that this book was written following the Second World War when thousands of mothers were happily despatched to factories and separated from their children without any catastrophic consequences. But perhaps her response was to be expected if she *did* base the book on her own personal experience of a 'deserting' father some forty years earlier.

Enid's attempt at social realism in 1951 is of a very different quality to current problem fiction, which developed at a rapid pace in the 1970s. Such books deal with contemporary issues like the problems of physical and mental handicaps, divorce and the urban poverty. In Britain, Bernard Ashley in particular has produced novels dealing with the difficult lives of present-day children in deprived urban homes, without himself falling into the clichés of the genre, particularly sentimentality. For example his *Break in the Sun* (1980) is a grim but subtly written portrait of a fat boy and a girl who wets her bed. In this story, Patsy hates her new London flat and her 'cruel, lazy' stepfather: 'There were wet beds, too, and hard smacks for her own good, and him only ever saying her name like it was a swear-word.' One day Patsy asserted herself.

> All right then! Patsy suddenly felt defiant. Let him be as horrible as he liked: she was going to have a bloody good try. Why should she miss out on everything? She walked to the living-room and stood in the doorway.

He's heard her all right. Now let him take some notice.

There he was, sitting in his armchair with his paper, like an up-patient in hospital, white-faced, small, and staring at her already. Deliberately, he folded the paper and tucked it between a bare arm and his white singlet, as if he were about to get up and go. But he didn't move anywhere. He hardly ever did. He just sat, as always: the lazy beast who even made you go and stand by him for a smack.

However, even in this more detailed and realistic account there is, as in Enid Blyton, a happy ending, when Patsy returns after running away. She is reunited with her mother *and* her step-father: 'His hand took hers, smoother than her mother's, and it firmly guided her away. Without a word he walked her back through the crowds and the pouring rain to a place under cover: a cafe where they could sit, and get a cup of tea...'

Perhaps these are the boundaries of problem fiction, perhaps 'reality' should not be forced upon children. However, as we shall see later, other children's authors disagree.

Enid Blyton's Magazine, no. 4 (5) 13–26 February 1957

ENID BLYTON: THE WARTIME YEARS

At the outbreak of war in 1939, Blyton's position as a children's writer was both secure and certain. In 1940 alone, eleven Enid Blyton books were published, including an earlier *Sunny Stories* serial, *The Secret of Spiggy Holes*, *The Children of Cherry Tree Farm*, *Twenty-Minute Tales* and *Tales of Betsy May*. In addition to the eleven, she also published a further two under the name 'Mary Pollock', both of which became popular. Barbara Stoney, some-what ironically, argues that 'the children who read these stories were not deceived' and wrote 'letters of complaint to Enid and the publishers'. It was eventually decided to reissue these and two other 'Mary Pollock' books under Blyton's own name.

During and following the war there were paper shortages and accordingly publishers' supplies were rationed. In addition there was the problem of blitz-damaged stock, all of which meant that it was exceedingly difficult to obtain new copies even of classics, like *The Water Babies*, *David Copperfield* and *Little Women*. Enid did not suffer from this, as her popularity, professionalism and business-like approach to the task of writing made her a safe bet for the publishers. As Sheila Ray observes, 'children born as the

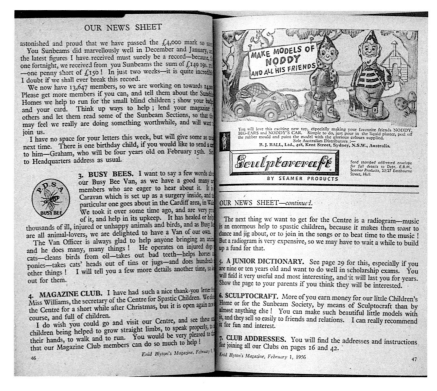

1930's wore on were less and less likely to escape reading Enid Blyton at some stage in their childhood'. Indeed by 1945 she was a most successful writer, with her books readily available in bookshops, newsagents and libraries. Sheila Ray, interestingly yet elusively, points to the minor but significant element of *chance* in Enid's success.

> One can see that it was not merely a question of the popular and meritricious driving out the good and worthwhile: there was actually a vacuum to be filled at the time where Enid Blyton was entering her most prolific period (she published 13 titles in 1940, 9 in 1941, 18 in 1942, 17 in 1943 and 22 in 1944). Almost by chance, it seems, her books were being published at a time when well-established children's books were not being reprinted in sufficient quantities to meet demand.

Again Sheila Ray is both quite accurate and in a sense poignant when she observes that 'having found a successful formula and an appropriate style by 1940, Enid Blyton's work changed little from then until her death in 1968'.

Meanwhile, back at 'Green Hedges', Hugh and Enid were still

Enid Blyton's Magazine, no. 4,
29 February 1956

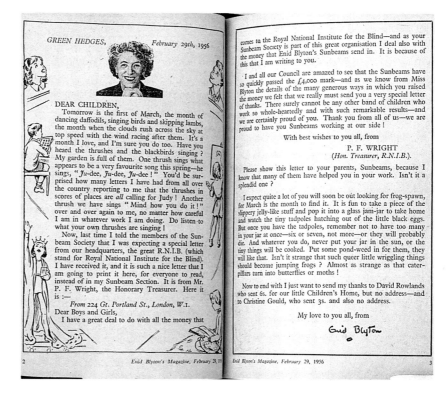

GREEN HEDGES,   *February 29th, 1956*

DEAR CHILDREN,

Tomorrow is the first of March, the month of dancing daffodils, singing birds and skipping lambs, the month when the clouds rush across the sky at top speed with the wind racing after them. It's a month I love, and I'm sure you do too. Have you heard the thrushes and the blackbirds singing? My garden is full of them. One thrush sings what appears to be a very favourite song this spring—he sings, "*Ju*-dee, *Ju*-dee, *Ju*-dee!" You'd be surprised how many letters I have had from all over the country reporting to me that the thrushes in scores of places are *all* calling for Judy! Another thrush we have sings "Mind how you do it!" over and over again to me, no matter how careful I am in whatever work I am doing. Do listen to what your own thrushes are singing!

Now, last time I told the members of the Sunbeam Society that I was expecting a special letter from our headquarters, the great R.N.I.B. (which stand for Royal National Institute for the Blind). I have received it, and it is such a nice letter that I am going to print it here, for everyone to read, instead of in my Sunbeam Section. It is from Mr. P. F. Wright, the Honorary Treasurer. Here it is :—

*From 224 Gt. Portland St., London, W.*1.
Dear Boys and Girls,
I have a great deal to do with all the money that comes to the Royal National Institute for the Blind—and as your Sunbeam Society is part of this great organisation I deal also with the money that Enid Blyton's Sunbeams send in. It is because of this that I am writing to you.

I and all our Council are amazed to see that the Sunbeams have so quickly passed the £4,000 mark—and as we know from Miss Blyton the details of the many generous ways in which you raised the money we felt that we really must send you a very special letter of thanks. There surely cannot be any other band of children who work so whole-heartedly and with such remarkable results—and we are certainly proud of all of you. Thank you from all of us—we are proud to have you Sunbeams working at our side!

With best wishes to you all, from

P. F. WRIGHT
(Hon. Treasurer, R.N.I.B.).

Please show this letter to your parents, Sunbeams, because I know that many of them have helped you in your work. Isn't it a splendid one?

I expect quite a lot of you will soon be out looking for frog-spawn, for March is the month to find it. It is fun to take a piece of the slippery jelly-like stuff and pop it into a glass jam-jar to take home and watch the tiny tadpoles hatching out of the little black eggs. But once you have the tadpoles, remember not to have too many in your jar at once—six or seven, not more—or they will probably die. And whatever you do, never put your jar in the sun, or the tiny things will be cooked. Put some pond-weed in for them, they will like that. Isn't it strange that such queer little wriggling things should become jumping frogs? Almost as strange as that caterpillars turn into butterflies or moths!

Now to end with I just want to send my thanks to David Rowlands who sent 6s. for our little Children's Home, but no address—and to Christine Gould, who sent 3s. and also no address.

My love to you all, from

Enid Blyton

engaged in occasional strife, and in 1940 Hugh took to his uniform once more. He rejoined his old regiment, the Royal Scots Fusiliers, and was posted to Dorking, Surrey in order to organise weekly courses for officers of the South Eastern Command on the use of small arms. Enid had protested, but to no avail. Later in the same year their marriage began to disintegrate.

While apart both had been never short of company. Hugh, for example, had seen a lot of the novelist, Ida Crowe, whom he had met in the summer of 1940. Barbara Stoney summarises the events with care.

> After the breakdown of a marriage, recriminations on both sides are commonplace and it is always difficult to gauge the truth, but Hugh told Ida years later that one of his staff at Green Hedges had given him disturbing information about the way his wife had been entertaining men in his absence — and to someone whose previous marriage had come to an end through similar circumstances during the First World War, such news must have come as a great shock. On the other hand, Enid also confided...at a later date that she had been upset by an anonymous telephone caller whose only

Enid arriving at Central Hall, Westminster, 1952, to open a Church Army annual sale of work. It was her first public appearance since an accident in which she was seriously bitten by a dog
(Topham Picture Library)

words had been: 'Don't let Ida crow over you' — a pun worthy of Enid herself. But, whatever the truth of the matter, their relationship reached a crisis point that Christmas, from which it was never to recover.

After Christmas Hugh returned to Dorking while Enid plunged back into her work, and sought 'consolation from one admirer in particular, who seemed only too willing to provide the diversion she needed'. More significantly, later in 1941, she took a few days holiday with friends and, at a game of bridge, met a middle-aged surgeon from London, Kenneth Darrell Waters. As Stoney reports, 'from the moment of their meeting, Enid knew that there was now no chance of any reconciliation with Hugh'.

Hugh did in fact return to 'Green Hedges' from time to time during the year, but before long they both agreed to divorce. In particular Hugh consented to Enid petitioning him on the understanding that after the divorce there would be no animosity between them and he would be allowed free access to his daughters. In the meantime Kenneth Darrell Waters' wife was also obtaining a divorce, and Enid was extremely careful to ensure that she herself would not be implicated. Enid and Kenneth, the happy pair, married on 20 October 1943, at the City of Westminster Register Office. Six days later Hugh married Ida, his novelist, at the City of London Register Office.

Once they had got used to it, Enid's daughters accepted 'Uncle Kenneth' as Hugh's replacement and also came to terms with Enid's decision to change their surname to that of Darrell Waters 'so that we can all be one family'. Hugh never forgave Enid for this nor, more importantly, did he forgive Enid for her repeated refusal to allow him to visit his children. The war distracted gossip column writers from the affairs of the Blyton household, and indeed when attention was once again focused on them Enid was firmly established as the 'devoted wife of a London surgeon, living with their two young daughters at Green Hedges — an image which was soon to become well-known throughout the world' (Stoney).

In early 1945 Enid once again fell pregnant, but five months later, following a fall, she miscarried. Life went on quite happily, however, with Kenneth taking a great interest in Enid's work. On the business front she formed her own company, Darrell Waters Limited (on 31 March 1950), in order to help coordinate her increasingly complex publishing and financial interests (like her purchase of a Dorset golf course). Previous to the formation of the company she had, shrewdly and competently, handled all of her publishing and commercial affairs.

In 1952 Enid withdrew from the magazine *Sunny Stories*, after

Enid at a 1953 schoolboys'
exhibition at the
Horticultural Hall, London
(Topham Picture Library)

twenty-six years as editor, just as she had seven years previously with *Teachers' World*. In place of these she produced her own *Enid Blyton Magazine*, with the first edition appearing on 18 March 1953, two months before the Coronation of Queen Elizabeth II, a circumstance 'which Enid was quick to follow up with a six-part serial *The Story of Our Queen*, and a special photographic competition with seats to watch the Coronation as first prize'. Stoney adds that in a later issue she 'suggested readers might like to send their own personal Christmas messages of affection and loyalty to the new monarch', which subsequently resulted in a 'special leather-bound volume, containing a letter from Enid and twelve selected greetings from the hundreds received, being despatched to the Queen'.

In addition to being a prolific writer of books she was, of course, both an engaging storyteller (as her daughters learnt over the years) and a writer of letters and articles. She was constantly being pressed for her views on all manner of topics, but especially those relating to children, and at the same time all her utterances were being recorded. For example, at the opening of an exhibition of mothercraft at the Central Hall, Westminster, in November 1949, she was widely reported for her criticism of the government's call to married women to work in factories as she felt this would mean 'abandoning children to the care of others'. (As we saw earlier, she managed to respond to this later in her attempt at social realism with *The Six Bad Boys*.) As for Enid herself, her own work took *her* away from the girls; they spent time at boarding schools or with nannies. But that, presumably, was a different matter.

In some of the early editions of the *Enid Blyton Magazine* she encouraged her young readers to follow a daily course of Bible readings, and in a 1950 Church of England newspaper article she talked of those who 'corrupt the young': 'I want to take up the whip that Jesus once used when he drove from the Temple the polluters of holiness and goodness. I want to whip out those who pollute the innocence and goodness in the hearts of children.' Enid also held opinions as to the country's leadership. Indeed in the *Sunday Graphic* on 19 March 1947 there appeared a poem, 'A Lion Once We Had', which she had written for Winston Church-ill, of which the final two stanzas read:

> If ever a man was England, this was he,
> Old Lion-Heart, whose heart was England's own,
> Leader of men, a Marlborough grown in stature,
> He stood for us when England stood alone.

Enid and family
(Topical Press Agency)

And now, when all our glory's dimmed and shadowed,
What would we give to hear a dauntless roar,
To range ourselves behind a trusted leader,
One for all and all for one once more!

She also held strong opinions about child murderers, dedicating a poem about them written during government discussion on the abolition of capital punishment (1950). Titled 'To Hang — or not to Hang — that is the Question! Two Points of View', it concluded:

And you ask me WHY I would hang this man!
Though you know it's our only hope
To stop any fiend who would rape and kill –
He's a coward — and he *fears* the rope!
You're not quite sure if I'm right – or not?
You'll think about it – alone?
Well, if you're doubtful, *I'm* certain of this –
You haven't a child of you own!

Although some people might well applaud her for her 'realism' (for that's unfortunately what it is), many would not regard her views as compatible with most forms of Christianity — not that she herself was very religious.

She may have held strong views on such matters, but she did not want murder, violence, rape, bloodshed or even torture or ghosts in children's literature — such things for Enid did not belong to the children's world. For Enid, it was perfectly possible to write any number of adventure, family or mystery stories without such events. And in so doing keep the child engrossed for hours. This she achieved, of course, with, for example, the 'Famous Five' stories, which became spectacular successes.

CHAPTER
— 3 —
ADVENTURING WITH THE
'FAMOUS FIVE' AND OTHERS

The modern adventure story, in its many variations, is directly descended from *Robinson Crusoe* (1719), a book imitated most famously in *The Swiss Family Robinson* (1812), followed by R.M. Ballantyne's *The Coral Island* (1858). It was, however, G.A. Henty, the most prolific and widely read of the Victorian adventure-story writers, who was 'responsible for establishing most of the clichés of the genre, and whose stories are certainly often guilty of racial and class arrogance', note Carpenter and Prichard (1984). Alongside such books was a much cruder popular genre, the 'Penny Dreadfuls' which romanticised the exploits of notorious criminals, together with the American equivalent, the 'Dime Novels.' In Britain, boy's adventure weeklies tried to counteract these publications, with the *Marvel* (1893-1922) and *Pluck* (1894-1916) prominent. Two seminal contributions to the adventure-story tradition were Richard Jeffries's *Bevis* (1882) and Ernest Thompson Seton's *Two Little Savages* (1903). Both books proved that small-scale and entirely plausible adventures could hold just as much excitement as more sensational stories.

In 1932 Captain W.E. Johns, a contemporary of Blyton's, created 'Biggles', who with his creator had little affection for most foreign races. As Carpenter and Prichard (1984) observe, a 'typical character in an early Biggles book talks about "Indians, niggers, and half-breeds, the scum of the earth"'. Our jingoistic hero, Captain James Bigglesworth, spends his time in combat and adventure, outwitting 'the Germans'.

> It was the largest aeroplane Biggles had ever seen. He noted two engines, one on each side of the fuselage, and raked his memory for some rumour or gossip by which he could identify it.
> 'It isn't a Gotta,' he mused. 'Dashed if I know what it

is, but I'll bet she carries a tidy load of eggs.'

Almost unconsciously he had been edging nearer to the nose of the big machine as he inspected it, but a sudden burst of fire from the gunner in the nacelle, and an ominous flack! flack! flack! behind warned him that the crew were on the alert and well prepared to receive

An adventure
(*Famous Five Annual: Five Go off to Camp* (1984) Purnell)

Biggles
(Captain W.E. Johns (1954)
Biggles: Foreign Legionnaire,
Hodder and Stoughton)

'Biggles knocked him flat'
(Captain W.E. Johns (1954)
Biggles: Foreign Legionnaire,
Hodder and Stoughton)

Biggles knocked him flat

him. He made a lightning right-hand turn, and as he flashed back past the bomber a murderously accurate burst of fire from the rear gunner startled him still further.

'Strewth!' swore Biggles. 'This is a bit hot.' (*Biggles, Pioneer Air Fighter*, 1954)

Interestingly, Geoffrey Trease comments that it may well be that in years to come the *Biggles* books will be read chiefly by 'half-incredulous research students, investigating the social values prevalent in children's fiction during the second quarter of the twentieth century'.

The USA's most influential contribution to adventure-writing in this present century has been the systematic creation of 'super-heroes', a process that began in the 1930s with *Superman* and *Batman* (both descendants of the Victorian *Spring-Heeled Jack*), and the production in more recent years of science fiction and fantasy films, such as *Star Wars* (1976) with Luke Skywalker, the dark lord Darth Vader, and robots Artoo-Deeto and See Threepio. Such films, of course, provide popular and easily accessible adventure stories for the young.

However for our purposes, in attempting to place Enid Blyton's contributions to the adventure story, the most important single writer was Arthur Ransome, who in the 1930s made use of the 'small-scale and plausible adventures' formula, most notably in his *Swallows and Amazons* (1930), the holiday adventures of the 'Walker' children. This book, together with sequels, led to the prominence of the 'holiday adventure story', in which children arrive at a country village or seaside resort and find themselves involved in the detection of crime, or in some kind of treasure hunt connected with local history. Carpenter and Prichard (1984),

'An adventure' (Serge Rosenzweig and Bernard Dufossa (1983) *The Famous Five and the Inca God*, Hodder and Stoughton)

somewhat unfairly, argue that 'the *Famous Five* series by Enid Blyton (1942 onwards) shows this genre at its most banal.'

THE 'FAMOUS FIVE'

Together with her little creation 'Noddy', the 'Famous Five' are, for many, synonymous with Enid Blyton. Certainly the books have sold in enormous quantities. The 'Famous Five' paperbacks have sold over twenty million copies, and continue to do so in many countries other than the UK – France, Germany, Denmark, the Netherlands, Indonesia, Portugal, Spain, Sweden, and many more. The books are clearly popular with the readership, as many surveys over the years have noted. For example, in the government's 1982 survey of 10,000 eleven-year-old children in 700 schools (*Language Performance in Schools*, 1982), Enid Blyton came out on top in terms of popularity — her stories were seen as adventurous, funny, never boring, and as always having happy endings. Although Enid Blyton's adventure stories were immediately popular with children of the 1950s and 1960s, they have since proved to be universally popular with the majority of children of a particular age group. Despite their obvious popularity with their intended readership, namely children, the 'Famous Five' have not met with anything like universal approval. Margery Fisher, for example, in her *Who's Who in Children's Books* (1975) describes the 'Famous Five' as consisting of:

> Dick, Julian and Anne and their cousin Georgina Kirrin, who always wanted to be a boy and who flies into a rage if she is called anything but George. The fifth member of the group, Timmy the dog, is addressed like a person and the children insist that he understands every word they say...thieves, kidnappers, spies, smugglers, are all powerless against their superior luck and their considerable skill in lurking and eavesdropping.

Fisher's primary criticism of the books is that the characters are insufficiently developed. She suggests, for example, that 'Anne's capabilities as a cook (largely demonstrated with a tin-opener) and her tendency to scream at sudden noises constitute her claim to personality', while Dick and Julian are to be distinguished from each other only by the fact that 'Julian is older and takes the lead', unless George dominates the situation, 'as she easily can and often does, for her temper, inherited from her father, is to be respected'. Indeed Uncle Quentin — 'such a truly brilliant scientist...has the finest brain I know...and yet loses some valuable paper or other almost every week' — provides the impetus for the adventures which inevitaby concern foreign powers and secret formulas. Fisher adds that, in her opinion, perhaps the most 'respectable reason' for the popularity of the 'Famous Five' stories lies in the 'variety and thorough-going improbability of the plots'. She concludes that in order to sustain a long series of

> predictably improbably and routinely exciting adventures it is necessary to draw characters impervious to emotion of any but the most superficial kind. This Enid Blyton has done most efficiently. Whether she drew her characters in outline deliberately so that children could more readily identify with them or whether she was simply not interested in character is a matter of opinion.

Certainly the characterisations are simple and the plots somewhat predictable, but this is the adult voice speaking, not the voice of the intended reader. Surely Elaine Moss (1986) is correct when she argues that 'Enid Blyton demonstrated that children are so hungry for *stories* that they will read the same story over and over, slightly disguised.' But more of that later.

Our intrepid heroes — Dick, Julian, Anne, George and, of course, Timmy the dog — made their debut in 1942 in *Five on a Treasure Island*, the first of what was to become a twenty-one book series, and which in addition led to the creation of one of

Enid Blyton's famous charitable clubs, the 'Famous Five Club'. In keeping with her style and her determined anti-research stance, in *Five on a Treasure Island* the geographical location remains a mystery; 'the children's parents decide to go to Scotland on their own, the children are told they cannot go to Polseath, which sounds as if it is in Cornwall, as usual, and this suggests that Kirrin Bay, to which the children are eventually sent, is in neither, yet to get there the children start from London by car soon after breakfast and don't arrive until six in the evening' (Ray, 1982). Sheila Ray argues that in *Five on a Treasure Island* 'we find the kind of incredibility which gave Enid Blyton her poor reputation'. Again this is adult criticism.

In any event, Julian, Dick and Anne's parents suddenly decide not to accompany them on the annual holiday, and instead send them to Uncle Quentin who, 'brilliant scientist' though he is, is a little hard up and could do with some extra cash. The children subsequently meet Uncle Quentin and his 'tomboy' daughter Georgina, whom a local boy Alf refers to as 'Master George'. She is clearly distinguished from the rather 'girlish' Anne who, unlike George, cannot row, climb or swim. Julian, the eldest boy, takes the lead to some extent while Dick plays a somewhat minor role. Uncle Quentin is seen as a bad-tempered, frowning, but brilliant scientist. Timmy, the canine conversationalist, takes part fully in the adventure and possesses a mind at least equal to

Five Have a Mystery to Solve
(1962)

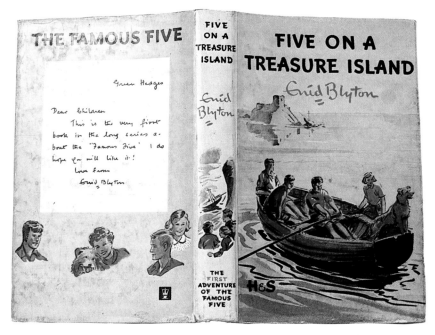

Five on a Treasure Island
(1942)

Dick's. The plot, despite 'its incredibility', is, according to Ray, 'well constructed.' Kirrin Island, home of rabbits and a ruined castle, lies at the mouth of Kirrin Bay and is one day to be inherited by George. Following a storm a wreck is washed ashore which the children duly explore, and find a box containing a map which appears to show the location a 'treasure'. The children have to overcome the obstacles of Uncle Quentin and 'the men who wish to buy the island' in order to find the treasure. They do so. End of story.

It *is* a simple style, but it has become second to none in terms of popularity. Mary Cadogan and Patricia Craig, in their book on 'girl's fiction' *You're a Brick, Angela!* (1976), put it well when they assert that Enid Blyton pushed the 'mystery' theme as far as it could go in one direction, namely that of simplification of style and crude dramatisation of content. They consider her approach to be almost precisely the 'obverse of Arthur Ransome's', who brought out the 'significance of commonplace childhood experiences', while she presented a string of 'significant occurrences in a way which is totally commonplace'. They sensibly conclude that

> She is consistently trite. She 'writes down'...Yet few children seem to resent this approach; the Enid Blyton combination of cosiness and excitement has proved almost irresistible, and parental disapproval and library bans have actually helped to keep her books in circulation. Their popularity has never waned.

For Cadogan and Craig the 'Famous Five' books' appeal lies in the enthusiasm of the characters and the constant sense of being 'on holiday' and 'in the thick of things'. More critically they argue that Enid Blyton's objective has been essentially 'philistine', removing layers of meaning and ambiguity, in order to present a clear and superficial expression of 'involvement'. Cadogan and Craig consider that *Five on a Treasure Island* contains one 'fairly strong character', and indeed it is George 'who has carried the series; the other three children are as unmemorable as the author can make them'. Certainly the difference between the two girls — George and Anne — is an interesting distinction. Anne is the stereotypical 'feminine girl'. In *Five Get Into Trouble* (1949), for example, she is stuck up a tree and witnesses Dick being man-handled.

> Anne was sitting absolutely petrified up in the tree. She couldn't move or speak. she tried to call out to poor Dick, but her tongue wouldn't say a word. She had to

'Should there be spectacles in the new edition?' (1942, *Five on a Treasure Island*, Hodder and Stoughton)

Five Get into Trouble
(1949)

sit there and hear her brother being dragged away by two strange ruffians. She almost fell out of the tree in fright, as she heard him shouting and yelling when he was dragged away. She could hear the sound of crashing for a long time.

She began to cry. She didn't dare to climb down

because she was trembling so much she was afraid she would lose her hold and fall.

She must wait for George and Julian to come back. Suppose they didn't? Suppose they had been caught too? She would be all alone in the tree all night long. Anne sobbed up in the tree-top, holding on tightly. The stars came out above her head, and she saw a very bright one again.

And then she heard the sound of footsteps and voices. She stiffened up in the tree. Who was it this time? Oh let it be Julian and George and Timmy; let it be Julian, George and Timmy!

She almost fell out of the tree in fright

Five Get into Trouble (1949)

Not only does Anne cry more than George, she likes to play with dolls (ugh!), cannot do 'manly' things, and also, most importantly, does not have George's quality of mind. Their personalities are again well differentiated in this passage from *Five Go Adventuring Again* (1943), where Uncle Quentin passes through the hall while Mr Roland is finishing the decoration of the Christmas tree, and comments in passing, 'I say — look at the fairy doll on the top! Who's that for? A good girl?'

Anne secretly hoped that Mr Roland would give her the doll. She was sure it wasn't for George — and anyway, George wouldn't accept it.

It was such a pretty doll, with its gauzy frock and silvery wings.

Julian, Dick, and Anne had quite accepted the tutor now as teacher and friend. In fact, every-one had, their uncle and aunt too, and even Joanna the cook. George, of course, was the only exception, and she and Timothy kept away from Mr Roland, each looking as sulky as the other whenever the tutor was in the room.

'You know, I never knew a dog could look so sulky!' said Julian, watching Timothy. 'Really, he scowls almost like George.'

'And I always feel as if George puts her tail down like Tim, when Mr Roland is in the room,' giggled Anne.

'Laugh all you like,' said George, in a low tone. 'I think you're beastly to me. I know I'm right about Mr Roland. I've got a Feeling about him. And so has Tim.'

George has a quality that appeals, *resentment* — the resentment that comes from her desire to have been born a boy. This dilemma surfaces occasionally, as when Anne, for example, in an uncharacteristic moment of spite, points out 'they're real boys, not pretend boys, like you'. (The question of why anyone in their right mind would want to be a male, we will leave unanswered.)

Five Go Adventuring Again
(1943)

Cadogan and Craig suggest that George's crucial deadlock has a force 'which transcends even the author's bland treatment of it'. Indeed, they argue more generally that 'character' is the least of Enid Blyton's concerns; 'the lightest indications of one tendency or another is enough to fit in with the lines of the plot.'

Of course another interesting feature of George is the question of the inspiration for the character. In her *The Story of My Life* (1952) Enid throws some light on the matter. 'Yes, George is real, but she is grown-up now. She had a dog, of course, and though he was like Timmy...in character, the artist has not drawn him quite as he looked — but then, she had never seen him, so how could she?' She goes on to add that the 'real George was short-haired, freckled, sturdy, and snub-nosed. She was bold and daring, hot-tempered and loyal. She was sulky, as George is, too, but she isn't now. We grew out of those failings – or we should! Do you like George? I do.' And so she should, for 'in an un-guarded moment, many years later, while discussing the *Fives'* popularity in France, she eventually confessed to Rosica Colin, her foreign agent, that George was, in fact, based upon herself' (Barbara Stoney).

"Beautiful!" said Uncle Quentin, as he passed through the hall

Five Go Adventuring Again (1943)

THE 'FAMOUS FIVE' FACE ANOTHER EXCITING CHALLENGE – CRITICISM

As indicated earlier, the intrepid adventurers have constantly faced criticism from those adults who concern themselves with children's literature. Cadogan and Craig argue that Enid Blyton ensures her readers support for the 'Famous Five' by using a number of obvious devices, for example, by developing the 'natural, but slightly anti-social' qualities of children — greed, intellectual laziness and conservatism — and presenting them in such a way that 'they appear wholly justifiable, even attractive'. Readers are told early on in each book a character's particular foible, so that this will raise a laugh when it is next referred to, 'and references to it thereafter are constant and plain'.

Bob Dixon, in his much-discussed books entitled *Catching Them Young* (1977), is one of the most virulent critics of the 'Famous Five'. He suggests that the majority of attempts to evaluate Blyton's work have, in the main, not gone much beyond the level of 'criticism of language and structure' in the stories. Dixon, rather, wishes to concentrate mainly on 'attitudes and values' in the content of Blyton's work. He concentrates his critique on the 1950 book *Five Fall Into Adventure*.

Five Run Away Together
(1986)

In this story the 'Five' are drawn into an adventure when some 'papers' are stolen from Uncle Quentin's study. Jo, a circus or gypsy girl (a status Blyton does not clarify), who is befriended by the 'Five', was apparently used in this robbery by her 'brutal father' and indeed later she is used in a successful attempt to kidnap George and her dog, Timmy. Jo's unloveable father is in cahoots with 'foreign agents' who have names such as Markhoff and Red. However, motivated by love for Dick, Jo helps the 'Five' and is (almost) accepted by them after 'she's been given a good scrubbing by Joan, the cook, and is wearing some of George's old (but clean) clothes'. With the help of Jo, the entire gang, including her father, are rounded up and taken away by the police. The story ends with Jo being adopted by the cook's cousin, and allowed to see the 'Five' sometimes, if she's a good girl. Dixon concentrates on an early scene when Jo first meets the 'Five'. Both Jo and George (as we know) look like boys and, furthermore, resemble one another.

Two people came slowly along the beach. Dick looked at them out of half-closed eyes. A boy and a man – and what a ragamuffin the boy looked! He wore torn dirty shorts and a filthy jersey. No shoes at all.

The man looked even worse. He slouched as he came, and dragged one foot. He had a straggly moustache and mean, clever little eyes that raked the beach up and down. The two were walking at high-water mark and were obviously looking for anything that might have been cast up by the tide. The boy already had an old box, one wet shoe and some wood under his arm.

'What a pair!' said Dick to Julian. 'I hope they don't come near us. I feel as if I can smell them from here.'

When they came back from their bathe the man had gone, but the boy was still there — and he had actually sat himself down in George's hole.

'Get out,' said George, shortly, her temper rising at once. 'That's my hole, and you jolly well know it.'

'Findings keepings,' said the boy, in a curious sing-song voice. 'It's my hole now.'

George bent down and pulled the boy roughly out of the hole. He was up in a trice, his fists clenched. George clenched hers, too.

Dick came up at a run. 'Now George — if there's any fighting to be done, I'll do it,' he said. He turned to the scowling boy. 'Clear off! We don't want you here!'

The boy hit out with his right fist and caught Dick unexpectedly on the jawbone. Dick looked astounded.

He hit out, too, and sent the tousle-headed boy flying.

'Yah, coward!' said the boy, holding his chin tenderly. 'Hitting someone smaller than yourself! I'll fight that first boy, but I won't fight *you*.'

'You can't fight him,' said Dick. 'He's a girl. You can't fight girls — and girls oughtn't to fight, anyway.'

'Ses you!' said the dirty little ragamuffin, standing up and doubling his fists again. 'Well, you look here – *I'm* a girl, too – so I can fight her all right, can't I?'

George and the ragamuffin stood scowling at one another, each with fists clenched. They looked so astonishingly alike, with their short, curly hair, brown freckled faces and fierce expressions that Julian suddenly roared with laughter. He pushed them firmly apart.

'Fighting forbidden!' he said. He turned to the ragamuffin. 'Clear off!' he ordered. 'Do you hear me? Go on – off with you!'

The gipsy-like girl stared at him. Then she suddenly

'An adventure'
(*Enid Blyton's Adventure Magazine*, 13, 1986)

Good Work, Secret Seven
(1954)

burst into tears and ran off howling.

'*She's* a girl all right,' said Dick, grinning at the howls. 'She's got some spunk though, facing up to me like that. Well, that's the last we'll see of *her!*'

Dixon argues that in this story, as in other 'Five' stories, the 'Five' never change – Jo has to make (superficial) changes to enter *their*

world. The readers, Dixon argues, are 'expected to align themselves with "The Five" and with the values which they represent'. In this story Jo moves from a 'dirty little ragamuffin' to
becoming a 'forlorn little waif', motivated largely by her love for
Dick. She's also deserted by her father and thus gives "the Five"
an opportunity to exercise their superiority and charity upon her.
The scrubbing by the cook Joan and the dressing up in George's
old clothes are 'an initiation into the world of "the Five" on a
symbolic level'. Dixon argues that the language Blyton utilises in
the 'Five' books is 'sociologically, middle-class based. It's colour-
less, dead and totally undemanding.' Dixon asserts that what
'overwhelmingly pervades every aspect of Blyton's work is the
insistence on conformity — and conformity to the most narrow,
establishment-type beliefs, practices and values'. The obverse of
all of this, of course, is that the working classes are seen in a less
favourable light. Indeed, as Dixon quite rightly points out, if the
working classes appear at all, they are seen as figures of fun, if
submissive to their natural masters, and only disliked and portrayed as rather stupid if they are rebellious. 'Gypsies and circus
people, and even the Welsh, represent greater degrees of devia-
tion while foreigners are, simply, criminals. They are all rather
less then human, as we saw in the case of Jo.'

In the main Dixon is accurate in his criticisms. Blyton presents
a lost world, of superior middle-class children against the background of a rosy England. She *is* disparaging about the working
classes and foreigners. And even her most interesting 'Five'
character, George (a.k.a. Enid Blyton), is never fully emancipated
– Julian always keeps her at a distance when the going gets really
tough. But is it so surprising? Sheila Ray is surely right when she
argues that Enid Blyton is very much a 'product of the period in
which she lived and wrote'. In the 1930s the image of the family
was essentially a cosy one. Children had moved to the forefront
of family life and parents believed that children should be told
'happy and cheerful stories'. Indeed, as Ray notes, it was thought
that many of the 'traditional nursery tales had a bad effect on
children and Walt Disney's cartoon version of *Snow White and the
Seven Dwarfs*, released in 1937, was thought to be frightening for
sensitive children'. This is not to excuse her obvious sexism or
her undeviating allegiance to middle-class values, merely to
understand her a little better.

Other critics have pointed to the *absolute* unreality of the
books. For instance, Nicholas Tucker, in *The Child and the Book*
(1981), notes how the children often have some surprisingly
impressive possessions. George, as we know, owns her own
island, while Tinker, a friend of the gang, goes even better: 'how
very, very proud he was of his light-house!' Tucker amusingly

Half a minute later Peter heard his father's voice.
"Yes? Who is it? *You*, Peter! But—but aren't
you still in the car—in the station yard? Where
are you?"
Peter explained everything as clearly as he could,
and his father listened to his tale in amazement.
"Well! Two car thieves going off with my car—
and not guessing you and Janet were in it. Where
are you?"

Good Work, Secret Seven
(1954)

muses that 'psychoanalysts have yet to analyse the treasure-trove of Enid Blyton's fantasy world, but when they do it will be hard to resist interpreting symbolism like this, when Tinker's most

Good Work, Secret Seven (1985)

A mystery begins
(1981 edition, *Secret Seven on the Trail*, Knight)

They saw a line of prints to the front door

treasured possession even puts Jack's bean-stalk into the shade.' Talking of sex, Tucker adds that although the 'Five' range in age from twelve to seventeen years old, there is never any sexual attraction between them to slow down the action.

Another, and in my opinion trivial, criticism of the books is proposed by Sheila Ray, who complains that the 'Five' do not 'actually age at all through twenty-one volumes'. Not only does this presuppose that a child will read *all* or most of the series, but it also begs a rather trivial question. Does it really matter within the context of simple action-packed adventure stories? The answer, of course, is 'no'. Ray also shares a feeling that somehow Blyton enjoys seeing children viewing the world in an almost omnipotent way – 'the adults are seen wholly from the children's viewpoint'. While Wallace Hildick (1970) goes further, and claims that Blyton gives her positive approval to children's cliquish, spiteful and intolerant behaviour. It seems clear, despite their good intentions, that both critics misunderstand Blyton, who was far more child-centred and populist than they could ever accept. Children, as William Golding has so graphically pointed out in *Lord of the Flies* (1954), can be horrifically brutish. Disapproval of such behaviour in literature is, to a degree, irrelevant.

The 'Famous Five' have gone from strength to strength in terms of popularity: a number of filmed versions have been made and the French publisher, Hachette, has published new 'Five' stories, based on the original characters, which have in turn been translated into English and subsequently sold in the UK.

Fundamentally, the 'Famous Five' books have succeeded because they provide easy and interesting reading matter for children at an age when they need to reach as much as possible to gain fluency.

'THE SECRET SEVEN'

Another huge Blyton success was another gang of adventurers and problem-solvers, the 'Secret Seven', a younger but just as fearless and clever gang as the Five. '"Well, those children seems to have done most of the work for us," said the Inspector, shutting his notebook' (*The Secret Seven*, 1949). In a thoughtless moment, Enid abbreviated the gang to the initials SS, when their first adventures appeared only four years after the end of the Second World War. As Nicholas Tucker observes, at school all 'the Secret Seven wore their little badges with SS embroidered on the button. It was fun to see the other children looking enviously at them wishing they could have one too' (from *Secret Seven on the Trail*, 1952).

Like the 'Five', the characters of the 'Secret Seven' are not

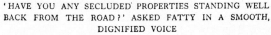

'HAVE YOU ANY SECLUDED PROPERTIES STANDING WELL BACK FROM THE ROAD?' ASKED FATTY IN A SMOOTH, DIGNIFIED VOICE

The Mystery of the Secret Room
(1945)

drawn in any detail. Interestingly, the series was first conceived by one of Enid's publishers, Ewart Wharmby of Brockhampton Press, who casually mentioned that his own children had formed a secret society in a shed at the bottom of his garden. Enid asked him for further details, and the result — with Enid as pragmatic and opportunistic as ever — was *The Secret Seven* (1949), a story about seven children and their dog, Scamper. In the end, fifteen titles in the series were published, with the final volume, *Fun for the Secret Seven*, published in 1963.

As indicated earlier, the seven children are almost indistinguishable from each other: Janet and Peter, at whose house the 'Secret Seven' meet, George, Pam, Barbara, Colin, Jack and, of course, Scamper the dog, who has a similar, almost human intelligence to Timmy, the 'Five's' friend. In the first story, *The Secret Seven* (1949), Jack, searching for his lost SS badge, sees a van arrive at a house which is known to be empty but for an old, deaf caretaker. He then hears some 'mysterious noises'. When told of this, all 'Seven' realise that 'someone is up to no good' and set out to solve the 'mystery'. In fact two men are hiding a stolen race-horse in the cellar of the house and are in the process of dyeing its coat so that it can be raced under another name. When Peter and Jack are put in the cellar themselves, Peter approaches the horse, rubs its nose and immediately the 'horse stood absolutely still'. The animal's skill is apparently due to his farm upbringing. The 'least credible part of the story', however, argues Sheila Ray, is the reaction of the parents when they learn that the boys at least have been out at night 'tangling with criminals: the dangers are never mentioned and parents express only pride and admiration in the achievements of their children'. What an incredible

'ARE YOU INTERFERING IN ANYTHING AGAIN?'
HE ASKED STERNLY*

'Are you interfering ...?'
(1945, *The Mystery of the Secret Room*, Methuen)

lack of imagination Miss Ray has! This is the stuff of the seven-year-old's daydreams: absolute escapism with plenty of opportunities for identification. The 'Seven' are *children*, and much of what they do is *childish*. The stories are as much about the games they play as the adventures they have: the adventures grow out of the games. And the adventures are adventures which only children can have: they can snoop without being noticed, they can stumble across a 'mystery' while at play. As Donald Fry (1985) so succinctly puts it,

> play temporarily becomes adventure, and the world becomes a place of incident, clues and suspects. It is also a place where children have status, where their interpretation of events holds sway, and where their actions have the power to straighten crookedness and end unhappiness. At the same time, the temporariness of an adventure allows the ordinary world to continue,

Mystery of Holly Lane
(1953)

The Mystery of the Secret Room
(1966)

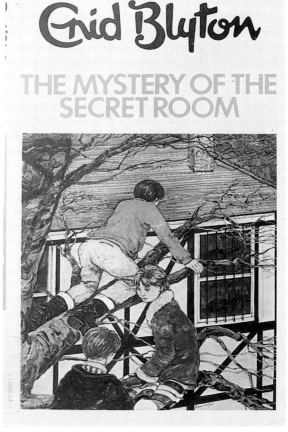

where children are dependants of their parents and are free, simply, to play. This is an attractive make-believe; and, although to adult eyes the Seven often seem arrogant and prejudiced, to children they are attractive because of their ingenuity and goodness and, simply, because they are children.

'An adventure'
(1982 edition, *The Island of Adventure*, Macmillan)

Indeed it is the two features of adventure and 'ordinary life', existing simultaneously, that make the books work for the child. The adventures take place against the routine of everyday life — rooms are tidied, meals are taken and homework is done. As Fry puts it, the 'Seven' are able to 'reconcile two conflicting interest, the need to conform and the need to be independent: home and adventure'.

The 'Seven' are not a likeable bunch: they often seem arrogant and prejudiced — and they are indulged in by friendly representatives of the working class, such as Larry at the garage, and others who express themselves in a series of expletives: 'Cor!', 'Lovaduck!' — but they are also obsequiously scrupulous about 'good manners', and would never dream of defying their parents. Peter, in particular, often reminds the others of what Mummy and Daddy have said: do not carve on trees, do put on your coat if you are going outside, do have a proper respect for books, do not take more than seven ginger biscuits! As Fry quite rightly observes, 'here are child characters who are a different breed from their young readers'. But as we have seen, the children simply do not see it like that.

'THE FIND-OUTERS' AND OTHER ADVENTUROUS CHILDREN

There is of course a tradition of more 'classic' detective fiction for children. Edgar Allan Poe's (1841) *Murders in the Rue Morgue* is generally considered to be the first true detective story, but in more recent times it was Erich Kästner's (1929) *Emil and the Detectives* which led both to many imitations and to the modern genre of detective fiction. First published in the UK in 1931, *Emil* tells the story of Emil Tischbein, who is robbed, on a train bound for Berlin, of money entrusted to him by his hardworking mother for the relations with whom he was to stay. A gang of boys about his own age come to his aid, and together they chase, capture and unmask the thief. The thief's guilt is proved, and he is discovered to be a bank-robber for whom the police have been searching. Emil becomes 'famous' and is given a reward.

The 'imitations' of *Emil and the Detectives*, in which groups of children outwit hardened criminals, range, according to Carpenter and Prichard (1984), from the imaginative work of C. Day Lewis (1948) in *The Otterbury Incident* ('regarded by some critics as a minor classic') to the 'formulaic and predictable' 'Famous Five' books. However, it is in fact yet another set of children, the 'Find-Outers', who are much closer in their adventures to the 'classic' detective story.

In *The Mystery of the Burnt Cottage* (1943) the five 'Find-Outers' — Larry, Pip, Daisy, Bets, Fatty and Buster his dog — believe a

The Secret Island
(1938)

(1975 edition, *The Valley of Adventure*, Piccolo)

local cottage belonging to Mr Hick was deliberately burnt down and they decide to find out who did it. They look for clues, assemble a list of suspects and gradually eliminate them: at the end Fatty deduces from something that Mr Hick says that he is in fact the culprit and the children then subsequently manage to work out how he did it and yet established a watertight alibi.

All of the fifteen books in the 'Find-Outers' series (a.k.a. the 'Mystery' series) are somewhat predictable and possess all the features of a characteristic Blyton adventure story — incredibly clever children with a lot of time on their hands in the school holidays. A central character in the series is the 'preposterous Mr Goon, a comic-strip policeman' who constantly attempts to obstruct the children's detective efforts (Cadogan and Craig, 1976). The following passage from *The Mystery of the Secret Room* (1945) illustrates the aforementioned features.

> 'Golly, we've had some fun, haven't we, being the Find-Outers? I hope we'll have some more mysteries to solve.'
>
> 'We've solved the Mystery of the Burnt Cottage and the Mystery of the Disappearing Cat,' said Daisy. 'I wonder what our next mystery will be. Do you think we shall have a mystery these hols?'
>
> 'Shouldn't be surprised,' said Fatty. 'any one seen old Clear-Orf yet?'
>
> Clear-Orf was the village policeman Mr Goon, detested by the children. He in turn detested them, especially as twice they had managed to solve problems before he himself had.
>
> No one had seen Mr Goon. Nobody particularly wanted to. He was not an amiable person at all, with his fat red face and bulging frog-eyes.

Cadogan and Craig observe that the baiting of Mr Goon often 'verges on the spiteful', while Sheila Ray argues that the children's attitude to Mr Goon is 'quite deplorable'. It is indeed interesting how an author as establishment-minded as Enid Blyton could have 'gone along so easily with this intermittent contempt for various representatives of law and order' (Tucker, 1981). But the matter is once again a case of Blyton's determination to see the world through the eyes of the child. As Aidan Chambers (1985) puts it:

> She quite literally places her second self on the side of the children in her stories and the readers she deliberately looks for. Her allegiance becomes collusion in a

THE YOUNG MAN, WILFRID, APPEARED

(1953, *The Mystery of Holly Lane*, Methuen)

game of 'us kids against them adults.' Nothing reveals this more completely than her treatment of adult characters like the policeman Mr Goon in *The Mystery of the Strange Bundle*. The unfortunate constable's name itself — chosen by the author, remember — indicates Blyton's attitude to the man, to his office, and her stance as one of the gang, one of the children in the story. Let's play this game together, she says openly and without embarrassment; let's have fun at the expense of the grown-ups; let's show them who's best; let's solve a mystery and have an adventure.

Mr Goon is ridiculed mercilessly in *The Mystery of Holly Lane* (1953) a book which, incidentally, contains the most extraordinary – yet presumably unintentional – illustration of a stooping Mr Goon and Wilfred, a rather camp 'young man'.

> That afternoon Goon arrived at Fatty's house. He asked for Fatty – and Jane showed him into the study.
>
> 'That fat policeman wants you, Master Frederick,' said Jane, when she found Fatty. 'I hope Buster hasn't got into trouble again!'
>
> 'Wuff,' said Buster, and danced round Jane. Fatty debated whether to take the little Scottie into the study with him or not. He thought he would. It might keep Goon in his place!...

and later on in the conversation, Mr Goon expresses his feelings.

> 'Ah, well, I'm a bit upset-like,' said Mr Goon, taking out an enormous handkerchief and wiping his forehead with it. 'Let's forget it. I don't want to interview you, but the law's the law. It's the last thing I wanted to do today – see you again. But I've got to ask you a few questions seeing as you and the others were the first on the spot, so to speak.'
>
> 'Ask away,' said Fatty, 'but don't be too verbose – I've got plenty to do.'
>
> Goon wondered what 'verbose' meant — something rude, he'd be bound! He determined to look it up in the dictionary when he got back. Verbose!

Enid Blyton wrote other adventure stories, including a series about 'Barney', which began with *The Rockingdown Mystery* (1949) and which are considered to be her most sophisticated. These books concern the holiday adventures of Diana, Roger,

Barney, who is a 'mysterious' boy with a pet monkey, and Snubby, with his dog Loony. (In her autobiography, Enid talks of her spaniel Laddie, who 'appears in many of my books as Loony': 'we often think that Loony would be a better name for him than Laddie, because he really *is* such a lunatic sometimes!')

Another series she constructed is the 'Secret' books in which *The Secret Island* (1938) was the first to appear, followed by such titles as *The Secret of Spiggy Holes* (1940), *The Secret Mountain* (1941) and *The Secret of Killimooin* (1943).

Sheila Ray (1982) describes *The Secret Island* as having both a 'survival' theme (in the vein of Defoe's *Robinson Crusoe*) and the classic Cinderella theme. Peggy, Mike and Nora, who are without parents (who 'disappeared on a flight to Australia'), are ill-treated by the aunt and uncle with whom they have been left. An older boy, Jack, who lives nearby, helps them run away to the Island. Despite the working-class origin of Jack's character, Enid Blyton does not patronise him, as he is both able – he can catch rabbits and fish, and collect nuts and blackberries – and soon established as the leader of the group. Peggy 'plays mother' to Mike and Nora the twins. The Island itself is an archetypal English one, with perfect features. As Sheila Ray describes it:

> the landing place is a natural little cove, there are caves
> for hiding in and for storing things and there is a
> spring to supply water. It has blackberries, hazelnuts,
> wild raspberries and strawberries and mushrooms for
> picking and there are fish to be caught. Since the child-
> ren are still on the island as Christmas approaches, two

'Philip gets a poor end of term report' (1982 edition, *The Island of Adventure*, Macmillan)

(1982 edition, *The Castle of Adventure*, Macmillan)

holly bushes are also provided. None of this is impossible but the ideal is provided in unlikely abundance.

Jack, Peggy, Mike and Nora soon attempt to create a 'paradise'. As Sheila Ray observes, the children are not unaware of the Robinson Crusoe element:

> ...one of them comments, 'An adventure! A real proper adventure, almost like Robinson Crusoe...' and later, when Jack buys a copy of the book to help pass the dark winter evenings, Peggy comments, 'It will be fun to read about Robinson Crusoe because he was alone on an island, just as we are. I guess we could teach him a few things, though!' Jack immediately assumes his adult substitute role to reply, 'He could teach *us* a few things, too!'

The book is centred on the survival theme. They survive both the threat of discovery and the ravages of winter, and manage to look after themselves. With Christmas approaching, Jack goes on a shopping expedition, hears that the other children's parents have been found, and we conclude with the family reunited in time for the holiday. Once again Enid Blyton magnificently captures the desires of children – her vocabulary may be short, but her ability to see the world through children's eyes and wishes is unparalleled.

Finally another best-selling Blyton series is the 'Adventure' books – *The Island of Adventure* (1944), *The Castle of Adventure* (1946), *The Valley of Adventure* (1947), *The Sea of Adventure* (1948), *The Mountain of Adventure* (1949), *The Ship of Adventure* (1950), *The Circus of Adventure* (1952) and *The River of Adventure* (1955). *The Island of Adventure*, the first in the series, following a slow start – unusual for Enid Blyton – moves into the adventures of Jack and Lucy-Ann, and Dinah and Philip, who track down forgers, robbers, gun-runners and other criminals whilst on their school holidays.

The 'Adventure' books are all marvellously predictable, as far as the child reader is concerned – once again, action, suspense and excitement. In *The Castle of Adventure*, for example, Dinah and Lucy-Ann are confronted by a man 'looking at them in the greatest astonishment and anger!' The man's face was 'not a pleasant one', as he had an 'enormous nose, narrow eyes and the thinnest lips imaginable', while 'shaggy eyebrows hung over his eyes, almost like a sheep-dog's hair'. Of course, being members of the 'weaker sex', as Enid liked to cast them,

The girls were terrified, and Lucy-Ann began to sob.

Jack, listening, longed to push the man down the steps and break his neck! 'Hateful fellow, frightening poor Lucy-Ann like that!' thought the boy angrily, wishing he dared to show himself and comfort her...

Philip, still hidden hin the suit of armour, took the opportunity of whispering instructions to the girls. 'Don't be frightened. They'll probably only think you're two silly girls visiting the old castle. You tell them that. Don't say a word about me or Jack, or we shan't be able to help you. Jack's up there somewhere, we know, and he'll look out for you and get away. I'll stay down here till I can escape myself. They won't know I'm in the armour.'

He couldn't say any more because all three men now came down the steps and into the hidden room. One man had a dense black beard, the other was clean-shaven, but the man the girls had already seen was the ugliest of a really ugly trio.

The Circus of Adventure deals with that exquisite image for the child, the 'kidnap'.

Then things happened very quickly indeed. Four shadows came from the copse of trees, running silently over the grass. Bill turned at a slight sound – but almost as he turned someone leapt on him and bore him to the ground.

Mrs Cunningham felt an arm round her, and a hand pressed over he mouth. She tried to scream, but only a small sound came from her.

'Don't struggle,' said the voice. 'And don't scream. We're not going to hurt you. We just want you out of the way for a short time.'

But Bill did struggle, of course. He knew what these men were after – Gussy! He groaned in anger at himself. This was a trick, of course! Old Aunt Naomi hadn't had a fall! There had been no real message from the farm. It was all a ruse to get them out of the house, so that it would be easy to kidnap Gussy.

(1979 edition, *Circus Adventure*, Macmillan)

Although all of the adventure series merge into one another, it would be wrong to see them as one and the same. For instance, the 'Secret Seven' books *are* for the younger reader and appropriately, the vocabulary is even simpler than in Blyton's other adventure stories. As Sheila Ray observes, for example, an ambulance is explained as, 'you know, the van that ill people are

*The Mystery of Banshee
Towers*
(1984)

taken to hospital in'. Similarly the stories of the 'Find-Outers' are more successful in structure than the other series. There are, however, extensive similarities: simple and easily accessible language, minimally-drawn and stereotypical characterisations, and all varieties of a somewhat predictable set of plots. Most important, of course, are the happy endings, for as Gillian Avery (1975) observes, in her *Childhood's Pattern: A Study of the Heroes and Heroines of Children's Fiction 1770-1950*, the:

> Famous Five and Secret Seven might have encountered every desperado on the Interpol calendar, but they know and we know that they are always perfectly safe. They can roam Dartmoor and tramp the fells in the calm certainty that when they are hungry and tired there will be a rosy-cheeked farmer's wife standing on her door-step, waiting to welcome them with cream teas and put them to bed between lavender-scented sheets. Everybody is their friend, except the criminals whom of course they will outwit.

Or as Eileen Colwell so famously remarked, in a 1948 review of *The Sea of Adventure*, 'what hope has a band of desperate men against four children?'

CHAPTER
— 4 —
LACROSSE, MIDNIGHT FEASTS
AND 'BEASTLY GIRLS'

In Britain the establishment of 'girls' stories' as a separate genre came in the 1880s, thanks largely to writers like Evelyn Everett-Green and L.T. Meade (pseudonym of Elizabeth 'Lillie' Thomasina Meade) author of *A World of Girls* (1886). Such girls' stories were set in boarding establishments for young schoolgirls. Perhaps the most well-known exponent of the genre was Angela Brazil (1869-1947) who when young, according to Carpenter and Prichard (1984), had 'fervent romantic friendships' with fellow schoolgirls which made her obsessed with schoolgirl 'crushes' for the rest of her life. Some of her heroines had somewhat quaint names, like Ethelburga and Avelyn, but her books are known predominantly for the language her characters use: 'What a blossomy idea!', 'It would be just top-hole!', 'A very jinky notion', and 'I say, let's play a trick on the prefects!' This type of language irritated many headmistresses of the time, several of whom banned Brazil novels from their schools as a result.

Enid Blyton wrote three major series of school stories in the period 1940 to 1951. There were three titles in the 'Whyteleafe School' series (the 'naughtiest girl' series) previously serialised in *Sunny Stories*, and six titles each in the 'Malory Towers' and 'St Clare's' series. All of Enid Blyton's school stories have remained popular and appear to be destined to sell for ever. One of the possible reasons for the fact that, even at their most routine, the school stories retain power is, according to Fred Inglis (1981), the *setting* in which the stories take place.

> The fact that so many of them are set in boarding
> schools has nothing much to do with class and the

alleged wistfulness of the poor to go to posh schools,
but has much more to do with removing parents from
the story, and providing a structure which promises
safety while making resistance attractive and under-
standable. The stunning snobberies of these tales,

Upper Fourth at Malory Towers (1949)

awful though they are, are unimportant to their readers beside the celebrations of friendship. The shape and meaning of the friendship is peculiar to the total nature of the little world the children inhabit. The school provides, as I said, stability and a clear demarcation of private and ethical space: you know where you are. It also provides a common work-situation, a common authority to be acknowledged and sometimes flouted, common rites of passage and membership.

'An Angela Brazil story' (*My Favourite Story* (undated), a collection of stories, published by Thames)

Enid Blyton's school stories are indeed located within fee-paying boarding schools ('although some scholarships are awarded') and *friendships* are central to the stories. For Sheila Ray (1982) 'Enid Blyton's school stories not only constitute some of her best work', they also 'represent a final peak of achievement for the genre'. Maybe.

Although the series of books as a whole is concerned with three different schools, one of which, Whyteleafe, is (unusually for the genre) a co-educational boarding school, the overall impression gained is – like the adventure stories – of almost absolute sameness in characterisation and plot. Which is not to say that they therefore do not work. Quite the contrary: the books allow an easy move, from one to another.

Enid Blyton's school books base themselves on the actual behaviour and the fantasies indulged in by schoolgirls at a young age. She works the stereotypes – but so do schoolgirls (and schoolboys) much of the time. She focuses on small incidents and expands them into melodramas.

Sheila Ray argues that as there are few stories set in co-educational boarding schools, Enid Blyton was something of 'a poineer' when she set her first school story, *The Naughtiest Girl in the School* (1940), in one. She adds that the reason for this was probably because the story first appeared as a serialisation in *Sunny Stories* intended for both boys and girls. Ray notes that the school, Whyteleafe, is run on 'progressive lines' and then, quite incredibly, Ray argues that 'those who criticize Enid Blyton for her sexism ignore the fact that the school is run by two women, with supporting male teachers'. Sheila Ray is clearly easily pleased. Witness, for example, the following conversation from *The Naughtiest Girl is a Monitor* (1945), between Elizabeth (who in five years since the publication of *The Naughtiest Girl in the School* has risen from naughtiest girl to monitor) and Julian.

'You've got to listen to me, Julian!' almost shouted Elizabeth. 'You've got to! Do you want all this to be brought out at the next Meeting?'

My Favourite Story
(*My Favourite Story*
(undated), a collection of
stories, published by
Thames)

'If you dare to say anything to anyone else, I'll pay you out in a way you won't like,' said Julian, between his teeth.

'All girls are the same – catty and dishonourable – making wild statements that aren't true – and not even believing people when they do tell the truth!'

'Julian! I don't want to bring it up at the Meeting,' cried Elizabeth. 'I don't – I don't. That's why I'm giving you this chance of telling me, so that I can help you and put things right. You always say you do as you like – so I suppose you thought you could take anything you wanted – and...'

'Elizabeth, I *do* do as I like – but there are many many things I don't like, and would never do,' said Julian, his green eyes flashing, and his black brows coming down low over them. 'I don't like stealing – I don't like lying – I don't like tale-telling. So I don't do those things. Now I'm going. You're my worst enemy now, not my best friend. I shall never, never like you again.'

It is appropriate to assess the three 'different' series as one, as the similarities easily outweigh any differences: all of the books share the same format.
– the girls *arrive* at their schools.
– new girls arrive and are immediately the centre of attention.
– 'heroines' are usually either given some kind of responsibility (for example, as monitor of prefect) or 'earn it'.
– we learn more of the 'new girls', and inevitably one of them turns out to be nice (although she could well be bad-tempered also), while at least one other turns out to be quite awful.
– the 'heroine' inevitably carries out some 'hot-headed' action but learns from her mistakes.

'You are a double-faced little wretch, aren't you?' said Darrell, scornfully. 'You know jolly well if you 'own up' – pooh! – that Potty [Miss Potts] will make inquiries and I shall have to own up to the spree in the pool, and the feast afterwards!...' At the thought of June sneaking on everyone under cover of being a good little girl and 'owning up,' Darrell really saw red. Her temper went completely, and she found herself pulling the wretched June off the piano-stool and shaking her violently'.

– similarly 'new girls' also learn from their mistakes, although on occasions one of them may have to leave as as result of her 'mistakes' ('"Shall I be expelled?" asked Deidre, panic-stricken at the

thought. "My father would be awfully upset. I haven't got a mother". *Last Term at Malory Towers*, 1951)
– a Jolly-ho ending: always!

ARRIVALS

At Malory Towers there is much excitement at the prospect of a new term of schooling.

(1945, *The Naughtiest Girl is a Monitor*, Newnes)

and so Felicity has the same first glimpse that Darrell had had four years back. She saw a large castle-like building of grey stone rising high on a hill. Beyond was the deep blue Cornish sea, but that was now hidden by the cliff on which Malory Towers stood. Four towers stood at the corners of the building, and Felicity's eyes brightened as she thought of sleeping in one of the towers. She would be in North Tower with Darrell – and it had the best view of the sea! She was very lucky...

Girls who had already arrived by car stood about the drive ready to welcome the train-girls. There were shrieks and squeals of delight as the coaches drove up to the magnificent front entrance, and swarms of girls ran to help down their friends.

'Hallo, Belinda!' shouted Irene, climbing down and leaving behind her night-case. 'Done any decent sketching?' (*Upper Fourth at Malory Towers*, 1949)

The next year the girls are back again, and in the same sleeping quarter, but this time the school is no longer 'castle-like', merely 'big'.

'Felicity! Look – there's Malory Towers at last!' cried Darrell. 'I always look out for it at this bend. This is where we catch a glimpse of it first.'

Felicity gazed at the big square-looking building of grey stone standing high up on a cliff by the sea. At each end was a rounded tower.

'North Tower, East Tower, South Tower, West Tower,' said Felicity. 'I'm glad we're in North Tower, overlooking the sea. Are you glad to be going back, Darrell?' (*In The Fifth at Malory Towers*, 1950)

Similarly at St Clare's, home of the identical O'Sullivan twins – Pat and Isabel – the start of term is not a time for sadness or fear.

The first day or two of a new term is always an exciting time. There are no proper time-tables, rules are not kept strictly, there is a lot of unpacking to be done – and best of all there are tuck-boxes to empty!

The twins missed their home and their mother at first as did most girls – but there was so much to do that

The Naughtiest Girl is a Monitor
(1945)

there was no time to fret or worry. In any case very one soon settled down into the school routine. It was fun to greet all the teachers again, fun to sit in the same old classroom, and fun to see if the ink-spot that looked like a cat with two tails was still on Janet's desk.

There were new books to be given out, and new pencils, rubbers, rulers and pens. (*The O'Sullivan Twins*, 1942)

(1986 edition, *The Naughtiest Girl is a Monitor*, Beaver)

PARENTS

Of course parents do have to be left behind. In her school stories Enid Blyton's feeling of resentment towards her mother for her father's leaving home surfaces in her characterisation of mothers and fathers. In this first passage from *The O'Sullivan Twins* (1942), a stepmother is used as the symbol for 'mother'.

> 'Well – there's nothing much to tell, really, I suppose,' said Margery, looking into Lucy's friendly eyes. 'It's probably my own silly fault. You see – my mother died when I was little. She was such a darling. And my father married again and my step-mother didn't like me. She said awful things about me to my father and he ticked me off like anything. I – I loved him awfully – I still do, of course, I'd give anything in the world to make him have a good opinion of me. He's so marvellous.'
>
> Margery stopped and bit her lip. The others said nothing.
>
> 'My stepmother had three boys, and my father was terribly pleased. He always wanted boys. So I was pushed into the background and made to feel I wasn't wanted. And of course I got worse and worse and more and more unbearable, I suppose. I gave my stepmother a bad time, I was so rude and hateful. And that made my father angry. So I'm the black sheep of the family, and I just got to feel I didn't care about anything at all.'

And Margery of course had been sent to boarding school as punishment. Lucy, 'taking Margery's big strong hand in her little one', listened as Margery explained that her father thought her no use at all: 'You know, he's wonderful – so brave and courageous. He climbed Mount Everest.' An astonished Pat cried 'Golly!', and added to Margery that she took after him, as she was 'so strong, and so good at games and gym – and so frightfully brave too'.

Darrell lost her temper

(1984 edition, *The Upper Fourth at Malory Towers*, Dragon/Granada)

'I never, never thought of that before,' she said. 'But I believe I do take after him! It's lovely to think that. Yes – I'm awfully strong – and I suppose I am brave too, though that's not much to my credit really, because strong people ought always to be brave. Oh, you made me happy by saying that, Pat. I think my father would think a lot more of me if he knew I was like him!'

Margery's happiness was complete when, a few days later – following a letter sent to her father by Pat, Isabel and Lucy – she received a telegram from her father.

Margery showed the telegram to Isabel and told her to tell Pat and Lucy. 'I'm so happy,' she kept saying. 'I'm so awfully happy. Fancy my father sparing the time to come and see me. He's proud of me too! It's simply marvellous!'

A further illustration of the fact that Enid based much of the stories on herself is that of the character Darrell Rivers, the heroine of *Malory Towers*. Darrell possesses many of the qualities Enid herself enjoyed – she spoke her mind, enjoyed pranks and was not unduly 'feminine'. In addition, the choice of name is significant, since there is clearly a link to that of Kenneth Darrell Waters, her second husband, whom she married in 1943. He, like the fictional Darrell's father, was also a surgeon.

'GOOD GIRLS'

In the school stories the 'good' girl is not the one who conforms, and behaves well, rather it is the girl who speaks her mind, is not too feminine, the girl who worries little about appearance, and the girl who realises it does not pay to be sensitive.

She was a very pretty girl, with curled red-brown hair, a rose-bud mouth, and big blue eyes.
    'A bit like that doll we used to have, really,' said Pat to Isabel. 'We called her Angela, do you remember? I wish Alison wouldn't smile that silly smile so much.'
    'Oh, I expect some one has told her what a sweet smile she has, or something,' said Isabel. 'Really she seems to think she's a film-star, the way she behaves!'...
    Every one grinned. They thought Alison was very silly sometimes. She spent ages doing her hair and

looking at herself in the glass – and if she had a spot on her face she moaned about it for days till it went.

'As if anybody would notice if she had twenty spots!' said Janet, in disgust. 'She's not worth looking at, the vain little thing!' (*The O'Sullivan Twins*, 1942)

Staying at St Clare's, everyone also found Sheila Naylor most tiring : 'she was always doing her best to impress people, and to make them think she was wonderful. Actually she was a plain and ordinary girl, with rather bad manners, who didn't speak very well. All her clothes were good, and she went to no end of trouble to buy the best of everything – and yet she never brushed her hair really well, and if she could forget to wash her neck, she would!' (*The Twins at St Clare's*, 1941).

At the co-ed boarding school, Whyteleafe, the presentation of self was similarly not especially appreciated:

The talk passed on to Arabella. 'A silly, empty-headed doll,' said Miss Ranger. 'I hope we can make something out of her. She really ought to be in the next class, but she is rather backward, so I must push her on a bit before she goes up. She seems to have a very high opinion of herself! She is always doing her hair or smoothing down her dress – or else trying to show us what perfect manners she has!' (*The Naughtiest Girl is a Monitor*, 1945)

'Getting to school' (1949, *The Upper Fourth at Malory Towers*, Methuen)

Other qualities were preferred: particularly stoicism and an ability to be self-reliant, to stand on one's own feet.

'Oh, June can stand on her own feet very well,' said Alicia. 'She's a hard and determined little monkey. She'll always find things out for herself – and as for taking her under my wing, I wouldn't dream of putting anyone so prickly and uncomfortable there! Wait till you hear her argue! She can talk the hind leg off a donkey...' 'She does,' said Felicity. 'Yes, perhaps you're right, June. I've often heard Darrell speak scornfully of people who can't stand on their own feet, or make up their own minds. After all – most new girls haven't got sisters to see to them. I suppose I shouldn't expect mine to nurse me, just because I've come to a new school.' (*The Upper Fourth at Malory Towers*, 1949)

SO UP THE STEPS WENT DARRELL . . . FEELING RATHER LOST AND LONELY

'Arriving at Malory Towers'
(1946, *First Term at Malory
Towers*, Methuen)

At Whyteleafe co-ed, Arabella was soon made to realise that the school would be no holiday.

> 'It sounds a terrible school to me,' said Arabella. 'I had hoped Mother would send me to Grey Towers, where two of my friends had gone – it's such a nice school. They all have their own pretty bedrooms – and wonderful food. In fact, the girls are treated like princesses.'
>
> 'Well – if you think you'll be treated like a princess at Whyteleafe, you'll jolly well find out you're wrong!' said Elizabeth sharply. 'You'll be treated as what you are – a little girl like me, with lots of things to learn! And if you put on any airs there, you'll soon be sorry, let me tell you that, Miss High-and-Mighty!' (*The Naughtiest Girl is a Monitor*, 1945)

Most of all it was the sensitive girls who were despised by such 'heroines' as Darrell Rivers of Malory Towers, who herself had no time whatsoever for such girls.

> Maureen's voice came shakily to Darrell. 'I'm always like this at first. I think of Mother and Daddy and what they're doing at home. I'm sensitive, you know.'
>
> 'Better get over being sensitive then,' said Darrell, shortly. In her experience people who went round saying that they were sensitive wanted a good shaking up, and, if they were lower school, needed to be laughed out of it.
>
> 'But you can't help being it, if you are,' sniffed Maureen.
> 'Oh, I know – but you can help talking about it!' said Darrell. 'Do go to sleep. I can't bear to hear you sniffling as if you wanted a hanky and haven't got one.' (*In the Fifth at Malory Towers*, 1950)

LACROSSE

Of course, one of the most effective means of overcoming sensitivity and 'getting on with the job of life' is to indulge excessively in physical exercise, which the girls at all three schools were encouraged to do. Such an expending of energy would certainly clear the mind of 'childish' worries and anxieties.

Malory Towers in particular had a penchant for instilling what it considered to be 'character' in the girls through such games.

Even two minutes was too much for the fat and cowardly Jo. Rumptious and brazen in everything else, she was a coward over cold water. She had begged her father to get her excused from swimming, and he had rung up Miss Grayling and informed her that he didn't wish his daughter Jo to go in for swimming if she didn't want to...

'I'm afraid not,' said Miss Grayling, in her firm, decisive voice. 'Girls sent to Malory Towers follow the ordinary routine of the school, unless it is against doctor's orders. There is nothing wrong about swimming for Jo – she is merely afraid of cold water, so the games mistress tells me. I think you will agree with me that Josephine should conquer the cold water rather than that the cold water should defeat Josephine?! (*Last Term at Malory Towers*, 1951)

'YOU SHALL WRITE ME OUT "I MUST NOT BE DEAF IN MAM'ZELLE ROUGIER'S CLASS" ONE HUNDRED TIMES'

(1946, *First Term at Malory Towers*, Methuen)

Being fat was certainly considered to be something that the individual girl was responsible for, as Gwendoline, also at Malory Towers, was soon to discover.

On Friday the doctor got a letter from the specialist and it made him smile. There was nothing wrong with Gwendoline's heart, of course, in fact nothing wrong anywhere at all, except that she was too fat, and needed very much more exercise. 'Games, and more games, gym, walks, no rich food, no sweets, plenty of hard work, and no thinking about herself at all!' wrote the specialist. 'She's just a little humbug! Swimming especially would be good for her. It would take some fat off her tummy!' (*Upper Fourth at Malory Towers*, 1949)

Meanwhile it was as a result of Felicity's determination to 'play on' in the lacrosse match against the Wellsbrough school that showed her grit and 'character'.

'Nothing much wrong,' reported the games mistress. 'A nasty twist – but Felicity's a determined little character, and where another girl would moan and make a fuss and go off limping, she's going to go on playing. It won't do the foot any harm – probably do it good'...

while later:

Felicity's ankle had certainly been black and blue the next day, and she showed it off proudly to the first-formers. What a marvel to shoot a goal when you had an ankle like that! Felicity was quite the heroine of the lower school. (*In the Fifth at Malory Towers*, 1950)

PUNISHMENT

Another side to this belief in the need to instil a somewhat stoical character in the girls is the belief that 'punishment' is necessary indeed not only necessary but almost inevitable. And, of course, like all schoolgirls, the girls themselves needed no encouragement in believing the same.

> 'It's a pity that cousin of mine is such a hard and brazen little wretch,' said Alicia. 'I don't actually feel she's afraid of *anything* – except perhaps my brother Sam. The odd thing is she simply adores him, though he's given her some first-class spankings, and won't stand a scrap of nonsense from her when she comes to stay.' (*In the Fifth at Malory Towers*, 1950)

Miss Grayling, the headmistress of Malory Towers, was certain that sooner or later, if a girl had acted in such a way as to deserve it, punishment would be waiting.

(1984 edition, *The Upper Fourth at Malory Towers*, Dragon/Granada)

"Don't you dare squeeze that sponge over me!"

> 'What do you mean?' said Darrell, half scared by the foreboding tone in Miss Grayling's voice.
> 'I only mean that when someone does a grievous wrong and glories in it instead of being sorry, then that person must expect a terrible lesson,' said Miss Grayling. 'Somewhere in her life, punishment is awaiting Gwen. I don't know what it is, but inevitably it will come. Thank you, Darrell. You did your best...'

Later on Miss Grayling expanded on her philosophy:

> Gwen stumbled out of the room. Miss Winter followed to help her to pack. Miss Grayling sat and thought. Somehow punishment always caught up with people, if they deserved it, just as happiness sooner or later caught up with people who had earned it. You sowed your own seeds and reaped the fruit you had sowed. If only every girl could learn that, thought Miss Grayling, there wouldn't be nearly so much unhappiness in the world! (*Last Term at Malory Towers*, 1951)

The girls themselves appeared to enjoy the whole roundabout and ritual of punishment, even when it did not progress as far as 'spankings'.

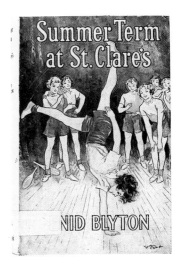

Summer Term at St Clare's (1943)

> June was angry and shocked to hear the verdict of her form – to be sent to Coventry for a week. She felt humiliated, too – and how angry she was with Alicia for giving Hilda the necessary authority! Alicia was quite within her rights to do this. When a member of a lower form aroused the anger or scorn of a high form, the head-girl of the offender's form was told to deal with the matter. And so Hilda dealt with it faithfully and promptly, and if she felt very pleased to do it, that was June's fault, and not hers. (*Upper Fourth at Malory Towers*, 1949)

THE WORKING CLASSES, AND OTHERS

As in all of Enid Blyton's books, the working classes and foreigners in her school stories, given a few exceptions, are treated in either a patronising manner or simply as objects of derision. This is hardly surprising given Enid's own background and lack of interest in understanding people other than herself, her family, 'children' and those in need of charity.

In *Last Term at Malory Towers* (1951), for example, her jingoism is to the fore:

> This was very naughty of Suzanne. No sixth-former would be silly enough to encourage the younger ones to come and play tricks in their room as much as they like – which was what Suzanne was telling them to do! But Suzanne was French. She hadn't quite the same ideas of responsibility that the British girls had.

At St Clare's, Janet was particularly concerned to correct Sheila's language, which she thought had dropped to the level of the gutter.

> 'You didn't ought to talk like that,' began Sheila, in a mincing voice – and Janet flung down her book in a rage.
> 'Hark at Sheila! "Didn't ought to!" Good heavens, Sheila, where were you brought up? Haven't you learnt

by now that decent people don't say "Didn't ought to!"
My goodness, you talk about your servants, and your

Summer Term at St Clare's
(1983)

> Rolls Royce cars, your horse and your lake and good-
> ness knows what – and then you talk like the daughter
> of the dustman!' (*The Twins at St Clare's*, 1941)

At the Towers it was Jo's father, monied as he was, who was the
butt of ridicule, especially from the superior June and her headmistress, Miss Grayling.

> Jo's father was rolling in money. Jo once boasted that
> there wasn't anything her father couldn't buy. June had
> inquired whether he had enough money to buy himself
> a few hundred 'H's.' Jo had never forgiven June for
> that. For the first time she had realized that her father's
> loud-voiced remarks were made all the worse by the
> way he continually dropped his 'H's,' and by his curi-
> ous lapses in grammar...

Jo's father Mr Jones ('Cheeky Charlie'), was also held in disdain
by another visiting parent, the medic Dr Leyton.

> Mr Jones was about to address a few hearty words to Dr
> Leyton, when he caught an extraordinarily icy look in
> that distinguished-looking gentleman's eye. It rem-
> inded Cheeky Charlie of one of his old headmasters
> who had once told him exactly what he thought of him.
> Mr Jones backed away, mumbling something. Miss
> Grayling sighed with relief. 'I'm sorry,' she said to the
> other parents. 'It was an experiment, taking Jo – but I'm
> afraid it's not an experiment that is going to work out
> well. We've had other experiments before as you know
> – taking girls that don't really fit in, hoping they will,
> later. And so far they always have done, in a marvellous
> way. I think Jo would too, if only she got a little backing
> from her parents. But her father always undoes any
> good we do here for Jo!' (*Last Term at Malory Towers*,
> 1951)

SCHOOL'S OUT...

The language of Enid Blyton's school stories is limited in terms of
vocabulary, at times quite odd ('But I honestly didn't know what
it was like to have slow brains. Now I do. It's awful. Fancy having
them all your life and knowing you can't alter them'), full of
expletives – 'golly!', 'wizard', 'gosh!' – and it is also the language
of the suburban middle class, of which she was, of course, a

member. In her school stories she shows the same degree of implausibility that infects her adventure books. However to the *child* it simply does not matter. Of course a child can grow out of the repetitive stories, and retrospectively criticise the books (although many adults reminisce warmly about them), but when read by the *intended readership* they match – even today – the daydreams and fantasies of the schoolgirl, especially those *not* familiar with the boarding school. The reader revels in stories of midnight feasts...

> 'Hilary! It's time! Wake up! Isabel! It's midnight! Joan! The Feast is about to begin. Kathleen! Kathleen! Do wake up! It's twelve o'clock!'
>
> At last every girl was awake, and with many smothered giggles, they put on their dressing-gowns and slippers.
>
> The whole school was in darkness ...
>
> At last all the eatables were safely in the dormitory, and the door was shut softly. The girls looked at everything, and felt terrible hungry.
>
> 'Golly! Pork-pie and chocolate cake, sardines and Nestle's milk, chocolate and peppermint creams, tinned pineapple and ginger-beer!' said Janet. 'Talk about a feast! I bet this beats the upper third's feast hollow! Come on – let's begin. I'll cut the cake.'
>
> Soon every girl was munching hard and thinking that food had never tasted quite so nice before. (*The Twins at St Clare's*, 1941)

(1950, *In the Fifth at Malory Towers*, Methuen)

Felicity collided with the big Wellsborough girl

...'practical jokes' and raucous behaviour: 'everyone went suddenly mad. Darrell gave a squeal of delight and rushed to Alicia. Sally thumped her on the back. Mavis sang loudly. Irene went to the piano and played a triumphant march from the pantomime' (*In the Fifth at Malory Towers*, 1950). At the co-ed Whyteleafe, the girls and boys also engaged in raucous, effervescent behaviour:

> Peals of laughter, roars of mirth, squeals and giggles filled the room from end to end. Tears poured down Jenny's cheeks. Harry rolled on the floor, holding his aching sides. Elizabeth sent out peal after peal of infectious laughter.
>
> It did everyone good. Those gusts of laughter had cleared the air of all spitefulness, scorn, and enmity. Everyone suddenly felt friendly and warm. It was good to be together to laugh and to play, to be friends. the first form was suddenly a much nicer place altogether! (*The Naughtiest Girl is a Monitor*, 1945)

Once again with these school series Enid Blyton has been able to write through the eyes of a child, realising that she had developed a successful formula, and proceeding to exploit it fully if somewhat predictably. Much of the character of the books is based quite closely on the manner in which *her own* personality developed, following her father's departure from the family home. The Towers' heroine, Darrell Rivers, is named after her second husband, she behaves like Enid herself and indeed is just as creative: 'Sally knew that the creative part had all been Darrell's. The words and the songs had all come out of Darrell's own imagination.' Girls at school should stand on their own two feet, be self-reliant and respect and love their fathers, who are seen as kind and charismatic. Their mothers, on the other hand, tend to be portrayed as either painted dolls or as somewhat 'hysterical'.

Enid Blyton's school world is light years away from accounts like Robert Cormier's *The Chocolate War* (1975) where, in a final scene, we witness raw, unadultered schoolboy violence:

> Stop it, stop it. But nobody heard. His voice was lost in the thunder of screaming voices, voices calling for the kill...*kill him, kill him.* Goober watched helplessly as Jerry finally sank to the stage, bloody, opened mouth, sucking for air, eyes unfocused, flesh swollen. His body was poised for a moment like some wounded animal and then he collapsed like a hunk of meat cut loose from a butcher's hook.
> And the lights went out.

Enid Blyton would not have approved. Her girls were proud of their schools ('I'll never let Malory Towers down'), and were turned out into the world as 'good-hearted and kind, sensible and trustable, good, sound women the world can lean on'.

There has been much debate about whether or not Enid Blyton's school stories are progressive or not in terms of women's equality. The writers of girls' school stories in the 1880s – Meade and Everett-Green, for example – wrote against the backdrop of female emancipation, yet they gave no real support to it and indeed implied that higher education and other such activities on the part of the 'modern girl' or the 'new woman' were just an unusual prelude to married domesticity (Carpenter and Prichard, 1984), whereas some current authors – Nina Bawden and Penelope Lively, to name two – present heroines who are 'complex, unaccountable, capable of irony, judgement, self-realization' (Cadogan and Craig, 1976). Enid belongs in both worlds. Her girls *do* go to university and indeed are encouraged to be self-reliant, but they are also encouraged to be 'sensible and trustable' people on whom the 'world can lean', – which is another way of saying domestic slaves.

Meanwhile, over at St Clare's, term has finished and school is out (*The Twins at St Clare's*, 1941).

Kathleen laughed and gave Janet an affectionate punch. She didn't live a great way from the twins and they had already made plans to cycle over and see one another. She was very happy.

The bell rang to say that the first coach was ready to take the girls to the station. That was for the first form. Shouting good-byes to their teachers, the girls ran

Upper Fourth at Malory Towers
(1970)

The Naughtiest Girl is a Monitor
(1986)

helter-skelter down the stairs and piled into the big motor-coach. What fun to be breaking up! What fun to be going home to Christmas jollities, parties and theatres! There were Christmas presents to buy, Christmas cards to send, all kinds of things to look forward to.

Pat and Isabel got into the train together and sat down with the others to wait for the rest of the school to come down in the coaches. Before very long the engine gave a violent whistle and the carriages jerked. They were off! The twins craned their heads out of the window to see the last of the big white building they grown to love. 'Good-bye!' said Pat under her breath. 'We hated you when we first saw you, St Clare's! But now we love you!'

CHAPTER
— 5 —
NODDY

Enid Blyton never appreciated or indeed understood the criticism of her work, and she famously held the view that it was
unnecessary to take notice of any critic over the age of twelve.
However from the 1950s onwards she *did* have to listen to a
crescendo of criticism centred around, in the first instance, her
1949 creation Noddy, described by Margery Fisher (1975) as a
'monotonously infantile, retarded, masochistic hero'.

Since his creation, his success has been quite incredible, by
anybody's standards. In total, Noddy books have sold over
seventy million copies since 1949, with our little hero visiting
such distant lands as Iceland, Spain and Indonesia, while in
France he sells (as 'Oui Oui') with almost as much success as in
Britain.

In her account of Noddy's origins, Barbara Stoney (1974) describes how in early 1949 David White, of the publishers Sampson
Low, Marston and Company Ltd, hoping to interest Enid in
another new series of books, and looking at some potential
artwork for such a series, came across a sheet of what he later
described as 'fantastically lively little people, beside tiny houses
in the lee of bluebells as proportionately big as trees'. He discovered that the drawings were the work of a Dutchman, Harmsen
van der Beek, whom he summoned from Holland and arranged
for Enid to meet. Stoney suggests that the 'first sight of Van der
Beek's drawings had excited Enid immensely':

> This tall, thin, rather mournful-looking man seemed to
> understand her own pictorial imagination and his
> vivid expressive illustrations both captivated and in-
> spired her. She immediately described the central
> character she had 'seen' emerging from a background
> that she felt '*must* be Toyland' and the Dutchman, with

Nodi (Portuguese)

112

Oui Oui (France)

'Noddy around the world'
Arabic

Noddy Bersekolah (Indonesia)

a curious, palm-uppermost style of drawing, sketched in pencil a quaint, toy figure with long ball-topped hat over tousled head – exactly, Enid claimed, as she had visualised.

Within a matter of days, on 21 March 1949, a small package from Enid arrived on White's desk accompanied by an enthusiastic letter.

I have finished the first two Little Noddy Books, and here they are. I have written them with a view to giving Van Beek all the scope possible for his particular genius – toys, pixies, goblins, Toyland, brick-houses, dolls houses, toadstool houses, market-places – he'll really enjoy himself! I don't want to tell him now to interpret anything because he'll do it much better if he has a

Noddys (German)

Nody en la playa (Spanish)

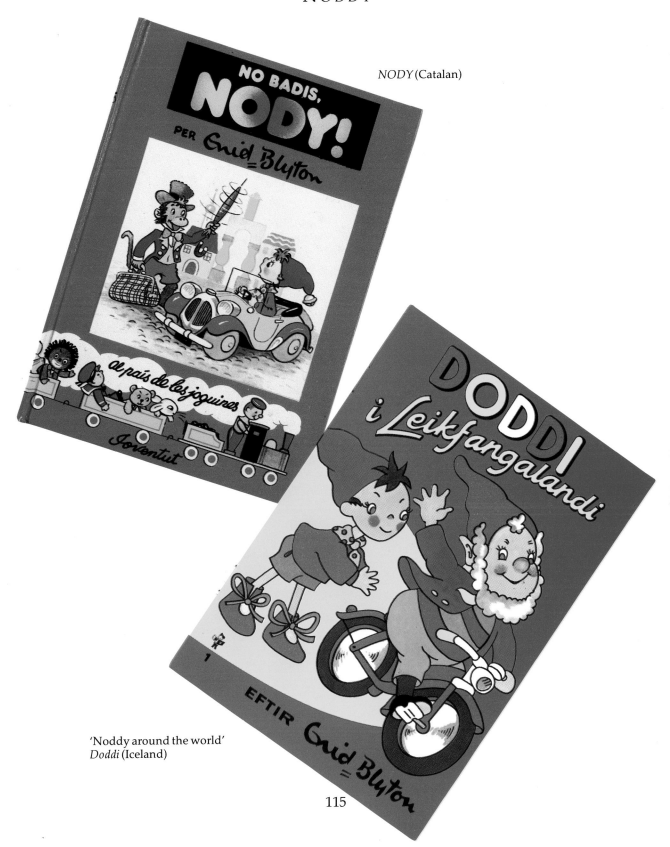

NODY (Catalan)

'Noddy around the world'
Doddi (Iceland)

perfectly free hand – but as Noddy (the little nodding man) Big-Ears the Pixie, and Mr and Mrs Tubby (the teddy bears) will probably feature in any further books, and will be 'important' characters as far as these books are concerned, I'd be very glad if he could sketch out these characters and let me see roughs.

Van der Beek duly presented Enid with some revised sketches, and later in the year *Little Noddy Goes to Toyland* was published. Its sales exceeded all expectations. Further 'Noddy' books were published and Enid was also contracted to write a daily strip series for the London *Evening Standard*. Van der Beek insisted on illustrating all of these but subsequently suffered from exhaustion in doing so. Indeed, as Stoney reports, he once 'confessed to David White that at times, when he was working through into the early hours to meet a deadline "Little Noddies" would appear from everywhere and crawl all over his desk' (Van der Beek died, suddenly, in 1953).

Noddy was first unveiled then in an extraordinary year: Britain devalued the pound; gas was nationalised in Britain; the People's Republic of China was proclaimed; the Soviet Union ended its blockade of Berlin, and also tested its first atomic bomb; George Orwell's *Nineteen Eighty-Four* and T.S. Eliot's *The Cocktail Party* were published; Richard Strauss died, while Rodgers and Hammerstein's *South Pacific* opened in New York, and we heard the song *Rudolph, the Red-Nosed Reindeer* for the first time; while the theatre welcomed Arthur Miller's Pulitzer-winning play *Death of a Salesman*. Noddy was also to walk the boards, the first occasion being in pantomime (*Noddy in Toyland*) for the 1954-5 season, the script incidentally having taken Enid two weeks to write.

Sheila Ray (1978) has argued that Noddy probably makes 'most of his impression on children because of the colourful illustrations and the commercial "spin-offs" rather than because of his adventures', and certainly Noddy did become a household name: 'Though a figure of fiction, fiction could not hold him: he became a hot commercial property. At different times you could find him on the West End stage ; on the back of breakfast food packets; on the handles of toothbrushes; and in the form of an egg-cup' (*The Times*, 29 November 1968). And today, much more besides.

'NODDY GOES TO TOYLAND'

Noddy enters the world of children's literature after he has a collision with Big-Ears the brownie, who is hurrying through the woods on his little red bicycle.

116

'You're rather a peculiar-looking person,' said Big-Ears, staring. 'What are you? You're not a pixie or a brownie or a goblin, are you?'

'No,' said the person he had knocked over, nodding his head.

'Are you a toy?' asked Big-Ears. 'I've never seen one quite like you.'

'No, I don't think so,' said the strange person, nodding his head.

'Why do you nod your head when you say "No"?' asked Big-Ears, still staring.

'Because I'm a little nodding man,' said the small fellow. 'My head's balanced on my neck in such a way that I have to nod when I speak...'

The little nodding man had run away from his maker, the Old Man Carver, as it was so *lonely* with him: 'besides – he's carving a lion now, and I don't like lions', said the little nodding man, 'I want to go and live somewhere where there are lots and lots of *people*.' Despite feeling sorry for him, Big-Ears is a little uncertain what to do with him; 'You're not a brownie, so you can't live in my town. You're not exactly a toy either – but you're very like one. You'd better go to Toyland.' So both rush to catch the train to Toyland, and on the way Big-Ears gives the little nodding man his name

'What's your name?' shouted Big-Ears, as they went along. 'Hey, leave go my ears! Tell me your name.'

'I haven't got one,' said the nodding man. 'What do you suppose my name ought to be, brownie?'

'Noddy, I should think!' said Big-Ears, nearly running over a fat beetle. 'Look out where you run, Beetle! Yes – I think your name is Noddy, little nodding man.'

'I think so, too,' said Noddy, happily. 'Yes, I'm Noddy, of course ...'

On the train to Toyland Noddy meets a couple of dolls, a wooden soldier and a pink cat – all intrigued by the newcomer. The train passes through 'Golliwog Town', and Big-Ears draws Noddy's attention to the 'dozens and dozens of golliwogs', and then it passes through other towns, including 'Clockwork-Mouse Town' and 'Toy-Cat Town'.

Big-Ears and Noddy get off the train at 'Toy Village' so that Noddy can get some clothes to wear. Big-Ears gives Noddy a short lecture on economic principles:

117

Original Noddy artwork,
1949
(Purnell)

4. WORK HARD, LITTLE NODDY

NODDY went to see Big-Ears after school. He drove to the little toadstool house feeling rather sad. Big-Ears was waiting for him.

"Why, Noddy, what's happened?" said Big-Ears, as soon as he saw him. "Your head isn't nearly so big!"

"Isn't it really?" said Noddy, feeling it. "Oh, perhaps I can get my hat on again then."

But no, he couldn't. His head was still too swollen. What a pity!

"Still, it is certainly going down," said Big-Ears. "School must be doing you good. How did you get on?"

"Not very well," said Noddy, looking gloomy.

Original Noddy artwork,
1949
(Purnell)

NODDY ISN'T VERY CLEVER

lamp-shades on his head. She ran after him and pulled it off. Then she gave him a spanking, which *Tubby* really ought to have had. Gilbert Golly howled.

"It serves you right," said little Noddy, who was watching, in delight. "You're a nasty horrid little tease, and you've often got me into trouble. Now you know what it feels like!"

Then Gilbert Golly ran after him and he fled. A-tish-oo! Oh, if only he had his own dear little blue hat back again with its tinkling bell!

46

this drawing has to be cut in two pieces. Please place the figure of Noddy, as indicated on the layout.

Original Noddy artwork,
1949
(Purnell)

WORK HARD, LITTLE NODDY

So he wrote all over the floor. Then, because it really was uncomfortable to kneel down so long, writing on the floor, Noddy thought he would stretch his legs and dance.

So he danced, and while he was dancing somebody peeped in at the window. It was little Master Tubby Bear from next door.

"Noddy! Whatever are you doing, dancing all by yourself?" he said. "Can I come in and dance too?"

'Now what kind of clothes do you want?' asked Big-Ears, who was getting very fond of the funny little nodding man. 'I'll lend you some money.'

'How do you get money?' asked Noddy. 'I don't really know what money is.'

'It's something you get when you work hard,' said Big-Ears. 'Then you put it into your pockets and wait till you see something you want. Then you give it in exchange. You will have to work soon, then you can get money to buy heaps of things.'

'I see,' said Noddy. 'Well, I'm strong. I can work *very* hard. I'll be able to pay you back quite soon, dear Big-Ears.'

They proceeded to buy Noddy some clothes, including his famous blue hat, 'with a bell at the tip that jingled'. Noddy's happiness with both his new friend Big-Ears and his clothes is short-lived however, as a policeman approaches him and sternly asks him if he is *in fact* a toy. Noddy, of course, is unsure, he only *thinks* he is. 'You might be an ornament', said the policeman, sternly. 'Like a china pig. That's an ornament, unless it's a money-box pig, then it's a toy.' The policeman thinks that there is nothing for it but to take Noddy before the court that evening, so that they can 'decide just *what* you are!'

Before his court appearance Noddy manages to build a house to live in, meet a friendly bear, Mr Tubby, and rescue a little doll from a lion. He eventually undergoes a gruelling court appearance, but in the end the court hears of his bravery and decides that he can stay in Toyland. The book ends on a note of optimism:

'I'll have lots of adventures,' he said to himself. 'Oh, heaps and heaps!'

So he will. I'm going to tell you all about them another day.

And so Enid Blyton does, time and time again, as we are introduced to more and more Toyland characters, including Tessie Bear, Mr Plod, Mr George Golly, Mr Nat Noah, Sally Skittle, Angela Golden Hair, Bongo (toy dog), Dr Bear, Whispers (Big-Ears' cat), Miss Fluffy Cat, Sly the Goblin, Dilly Duck, Little Ears (Big-Ears' brother), Hee Haw the Donkey, Miss Thimble Doll, Wobbly Woman, Sid Golly, Mr Honk, Katie Kangaroo, Wily Wizard, Mermaids and Mermen, Mickey Monkey, Mr and Mrs Tootle (gypsies) and their children the Little Toots, Katie Kettle, and many, many more.

NODDY – CHARLIE CHAPLIN OR NORMAN WISDOM?

Colin Welch, in an article entitled 'Dear Little Noddy', published in 1958 in the journal *Encounter*, mercilessly criticised Enid's creation. His article had a snowballing effect. Welch begins by asserting that the 'Noddy business' has by now taken its place among Britain's major non-warlike industries, along with 'sauce bottling, the pools, cheesecake photography and the manufacture of ice lollies, righteous indignation, and plastic pixies'. Acidly he adds that Noddy books are 'not enjoyed by grown-ups and forced upon children: they are enjoyed by children and forced upon grown-ups', and that the 'story behind practically every copy sold is of a delighted child and an adult's dead body.' More specifically Welch argues that:

> By writing ruthlessly *down* to children, she does not merely bore and antagonise grown-ups. Her Noddy books also fail to stretch the imagination of children, to enlarge their experience, to kindle wonder in them or awaken their delight in words. They contain nothing incomprehensible even to the dimmest child, nothing mysterious or stimulating...By putting everything within reach of the child's mind, they enervate and cripple it.

According to Welch, Blyton saw her Noddy as a 'helpless little man who gets into trouble and invites sympathy – a children's version of the early Charlie Chaplin'. Welch, on the other hand, sees more of a resemblance to the 'mature Norman Wisdom', and comments that Noddy's 'imbecility is almost indecent'. On our hero's nodding head, Welch argues that:

> The clinical explanation of this palsy or St Vitus's dance is that the victim's head is supported by a spring. Yet, in the light of Noddy's manifest feeble-mindedness, it is bound to acquire a deeper and more sinister significance. One recalls Zinsser's description of St John's Evil, a medieval scourge in which whole villages, driven mad by want and misery, went about shaking and nodding.

But Welch does not stop there. More striking even than Noddy's imbecility, Welch argues, is his timidity, which again 'borders on the pathological'. He adds that in some respects, the Noddy

121

books give the impression of being an 'unintentional yet not wholly inaccurate satire on – or parody of – the welfare state and its attendant attitudes of mind'. Welch considered that Noddy was particularly deplorable, on the grounds that he seemed incapable of looking after himself and was always running to Big-Ears for help.

Welch concludes that if Noddy is 'like the children themselves' (as Enid Blyton claimed), it is the 'most unpleasant child that he most resembles' – he is 'querulous, irritable, and humourless': 'In this witless, spiritless, snivelling, sneaking doll the children of England are expected to find themselves reflected.'

However, it was not Noddy's alleged imbecility or timidity that led to the most damaging criticisms, rather it was the accusations of racism made by many, particularly concerning the golliwogs in Noddy books.

Leslie Sarany seen with Enid Blyton at the final rehearsal of *Noddy in Toyland*, 1955, Princes Theatre, left
(The Photo Source)

Colin Spaull plays Noddy and Gloria Johnson plays Silky in *Noddy in Toyland*, 1957
(The Photo Source)

RACISM

It *is* important not to perpetuate racism by drawing misleading stereotypes of cultures and races in literature. But it is also, as Bob Dixon quite rightly points out, difficult in children's literature (especially that intended for the very young) to *combat* racism, as such tendencies tend to work on a symbolic and unconscious level. As he puts it, it is 'difficult to combat racism instilled in this way by argument, as small children aren't able to cope with the necessary ideas.' He adds that it is only possible to combat such racism effectively through literature for children which 'embodies civilised attitudes carried at the same emotional and symbolic level'.

Noddy with hens
(1965, *Learn to Read About Animals with Noddy*, Sampson Low)

Page one of *Noddy in Toyland* (1954)

ACT ONE

Scene One

The Scene is set in Toyland Village, where Little Noddy lives. (See pictures from the Little Noddy Books to show what kind of houses, etc. there should be.) Upstage is a cut-out wall running from left to right about 3'6" high, to the right side of which, as if in the distance, is the prow of a Noah's Ark. The wall is gaily decorated. In front of it are cut-outs of houses with practical doors and windows. If possible there should be at least three separate houses including Noddy's and Mr. Tubby Bear's and also Mr. Plod the Policeman's Police-Station. The whole scene looks lively, colourful and gay. Lamp-posts are here and there, and MR. PLOD is in the middle of the wide thoroughfare directing the traffic. Toys go about their business, chattering and laughing, doing their shopping, riding small bicycles or tricycles and so on. They sing the Opening Chorus:-

OPENING SONG: TOYLAND VILLAGE

VERSE:

Come to Toyland and you'll meet
Lots of toys in every street,
Little dolls with curly hair
And a nice fat Teddy Bear.
Wobbly men you're sure to see,
Skittles going home to tea,
Coloured balls that bounce up high,
Wooden soldiers marching by.

REFRAIN:

Oh sing the song of Toyland Town
With a Hey derry, Ho derry, Hey!
Where toys go up the street and down,
With a Hey derry, Ho derry, Hey!
The animals out of Noah's Ark
Come chattering two by two
And all day long
They sing this song
Hey derry, Ho derry, Hey, Hey, Hey!
With a Hey derry, Ho derry, Hey!

(Repeat)

As Elaine Moss (1986) has argued, the 1970s were years in which 'Britain was coming to terms with its post-Imperial role as a multicultural nation' and this had its effect on the content of the books children were offered. The editors of *Children's Books for a Multi-Cultural Society* (1985) argue that unless 'we want our children to develop an inward-looking, insular perspective, educating them for the future must imply educating them to live in and play a positive role in a society where cultural diversity is recognised and respected'. Children of all ages, they add, have

BIG-EARS GETS A SURPRISE

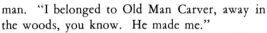

man. "I belonged to Old Man Carver, away in the woods, you know. He made me."

"Did he really?" said Big-Ears. "How did he make you?"

Noddy meets Big-Ears
(1949, *Noddy Goes to Toyland*, Purnell)

Gollywogs
(1949, *Noddy Goes to Toyland*, Purnell)

the 'right to a body of literature which reflects naturally the varied experiences and rich cultural diversity of the people who together make up our society'. In particular they argue that we should look for

– books that reflect a multi-cultural world in an accurate and balanced way

– books in which people from all ethnic groups are shown in everyday activities and sharing common experiences

– books in which children and adults from all ethnic groups in Britain are shown as positive people, taking responsibility, making decisions, being successful, respected and admired

– books which make it possible to feel what it is like to belong to another ethnic or cultural group.

So far so good. One particular problem which faces those concerned to produce such books is the question of how to treat racism itself in children's literature. As Moss observes, Jan Needle tackles the problems faced by an immigrant Pakistani family in Bradford in *My Mate Shofiq* (1979), a book that offended

THE ENID BLYTON STORY

IS NODDY A TOY, OR NOT ?

Then everyone clapped and stamped and cheered loudly. The judge rapped his table again. He was smiling.

"Ah—that's a nice thing to hear!" he said. "Noddy *is* a toy. He's a *good* toy. He's a *brave* toy! Noddy, you can live in Toyland, and have the house you built!"

Well, wasn't that lovely? Big-Ears laughed and shouted, and thumped Noddy on the back. Everyone crowded round him.

some 'white liberal guideline-addicts because abusive epithets were not edited out of the dialogue'. We were being asked, she argues, to 'present a realistic picture of Pakistani experience in Bradford without showing the hero's subjection to the unsavoury nicknames that were part of the reality'.

Noddy on trial
(1949, *Noddy Goes to Toyland*)

Noddy and his friends celebrate
(1949, *Noddy Goes to Toyland*)

'LITTLE BLACK SAMBO', AND THE 'LITTLE BLACK DOLL'

A particularly well-known example of alleged racism in children's literature, pre-dating Enid Blyton, is Helen Bannerman's (1899) *The Story of Little Black Sambo*. Bannerman, born in Edinburgh, married an army doctor, lived with him in India and wrote *Little Black Sambo* while travelling between Madras and the hill-station where her two daughters were staying during the hot season. The book's numerous critics have argued that the family

126

are shown as greedy (Little Black Sambo eats 169 pancakes, because he is so hungry), happy, clownish, indeed 'irresponsible plantation niggers'. (Incidentally Bannerman also seems to mix up her races, unwittingly.) Roald Dahl's (1964) *Charlie and the Chocolate Factory*, W.E. Johns's *Biggles* books and Hugh Lofting's *Doctor Dolittle* books are amongst other notable books accused of racism.

Enid Blyton has been condemned as racist not only on the grounds of the Noddy books, but others also. *Little Black Doll* (1949) has been described by Janet Hill (1977) as the 'supreme' example of 'blatant racialism'. In the story a little black doll, also called Sambo, with 'tight curly black hair' and a 'smile that showed his very white teeth', was sad because the other toys in the nursery did not like him.

> 'Why don't you like me, please tell me why?' he asked anxiously, for he very much wanted to be friendly.
> 'Well, you see, you're black,' said the big teddy bear.
> 'Why shouldn't I be?' asked Sambo astonished. 'The

ONE day Mrs. Tubby Bear met Big-Ears, and they talked about little Noddy. "You spoil him," Mrs. Tubby said. "He's much too babyish."

"He's not!" said Big-Ears, crossly, and marched off to find Noddy. Noddy rushed to meet him, caught his foot on a stone and fell over, bang!

And there he was, sitting down on the path, wailing. "Get up!" said Big-Ears. "You're not hurt! You can't be, because you've a wooden body!"

Noddy got up. He pulled up his shorts and showed Big-Ears his leg. "I'm dented a bit here," he said. "You just look and see, Big-Ears."

"Don't be a baby!" said Big-Ears. "Come along, let's go to the farm and get some eggs." So here they go together, down the little lane.

Noddy runs on ahead, skipping and jumping—but what's this looking through the hedge from the other side of the field? Oooooh —what is it?

Noddy the cry-baby (1952)

"Don't be ashamed of me!" said Noddy, getting out his hanky. "You're upsetting me, Big-Ears. I shall cry a big puddle of tears now."

Big-Ears stared at him. Dear, dear, Mrs. Tubby was right. Noddy had been spoilt. He was a silly little baby! Look at the puddle of tears!

"You want a spanking!" said Big-Ears, rolling up his sleeves and looking fierce. "Come here!" But Noddy ran away as fast as he could.

Noddy ran back, yelling to Big-Ears. "Big-Ears, Big-Ears, save me. A horrid creature looked through the hedge and roared at me. Save me!"

What do you think it was? An old cow belonging to Farmer Straw! She had poked her head through the hedge and mooed loudly!

"Noddy! Don't be so silly!" said Big-Ears. "Fancy running away from a poor old cow! And it mooed, it didn't roar. I'm ashamed of you."

golliwog's black, too, but you like him.'

'Golliwogs always *are* black,' said the baby doll. 'We wouldn't like them if they weren't. But dolls aren't supposed to be black. You look queer to us.'

Sambo was further dismayed: 'Well, I can't do anything about that,' he said. 'I was made black, and I suppose I must always be black. It's most unlucky for me.' Sambo thought he would 'try and make up for his blackness by being very unselfish and kind'. This altruism didn't work either, so he resigned himself to never being liked and decided to run away. He wasn't very good at running away either, and ended up lost in the grass, in pouring rain. Meanwhile the other nursery toys – the clockwork mouse, the golliwog, the golden-haired doll and the bear – decided they *did* like him after all.

'I'm going to find him,' said the golly, suddenly. All the toys thought they would like to go too, so they climbed up to the window-sill and out into the garden.

128

NODDY

It wasn't very long before they found little Sambo, lying in the rain on the big tennis lawn. They picked him up and helped him to hobble back home. He was very wet and very cold and he sneezed a lot.

'I ran away,' he said. 'I can't bear you not to like me. I can't help being black.'

'We do like you,' said the golly. 'We like you very much. We were silly. You just come back and live with us again and see how much we like you.'

Now when they were all back in the nursery the toys had a great shock. They looked at the little black doll – and he wasn't black any more! The rain had washed his face quite white. He did look queer.

Now it's time to draw and paint,
And make a picture gay.
I'll hang the good ones on the wall,
So do your best today.

Bunny Rabbit, stand up, please,
You've painted yourself YELLOW!
You shan't go out to play today,
You naughty little fellow!

Noddy in the classroom (1952, *A Day at School With Noddy*)

Poor Sambo thought that this was in fact good – 'now perhaps you won't dislike me because I am black'.

'But I want you to be black!' said the clockwork mouse, almost crying. 'You don't look like Sambo any more. It was Black Sambo I liked. I want Black Sambo back again.' All the toys felt the same. It was funny. They stared at White Sambo, and longed for him to be black again, the little smiling black doll they had known so well.

Sambo realised he was in a Catch-22 position: 'This is dreadful', said Sambo. First I'm black and you don't like me. Then I get white, and you still don't like me. I am very unhappy.' At that moment, the golly – who had clearly been in the nursery longer than Sambo – had a brainwave.

'Listen,' said the golly, suddenly. 'There is some black ink in the ink-pot. Let me get a rag, Sambo, and dip it into the ink and rub your face with it. Then you'll be black again and we shall like you.'

So the golliwog took a bit of rag from the paint-box, dipped it into the ink and rubbed Sambo's face with it. In a trice he was black again. His eyes shone, his teeth shone, and he smiled as he had always smiled.

The golly hugged him. The mouse wrapped his tail round his leg. The baby doll kissed him. The bear squeezed him. He was their own little black Sambo once more!

'Now do you like me again?' asked Sambo.

'We don't like you because you are black or because you are white,' said the golly. 'We like you because you

Little Black Sambo
(Helen Bannerman (orig.
1899), *The Story of Little Black
Sambo*, Chatto and Windus)

are kind and friendly and good. You can be any colour you like. We don't really care. Don't you dare to run away again, or we shall be very unhappy.'

'I shall never run away if you are my friends,' said Sambo, happily. And he never did.

A happy ending perhaps, but a very demoralising tale nevertheless.

Another Blyton story which has been considered offensive is *The Three Golliwogs* (1944), which featured 'three gollies' named 'Golly, Woggie, and Nigger'. In one story, 'The Three Gollies up a Tree!', a man trying to help one of the golliwogs stuck up a tree, meets the other, but thinks it really is the same one playing tricks on him.

> Mister Fussy looked up. He saw a golly on the ground. He saw another on one side of him, and a third on the other – and they all looked exactly alike!
>
> 'It's a bad dream!' he shouted. 'One golly has turned into three! Help! Help! Help!'
>
> And he tore off at top speed, leaving the three gollies staring after him in astonishment.
>
> Poor Mister Fussy! He did his best, didn't he! He always runs away when he sees a golliwog now – and really, I'm not surprised.

Such stories, and such language and description, would, quite rightly, be totally unacceptable today. However, Sheila Ray (1982) is also correct in suggesting that Enid Blyton, like Helen Bannerman, was writing for a 'very different kind of society from the one in which today's children live', and that the 'attitudes which

Little Black Sambo at the
meal table
(Helen Bannerman (orig.
1899), *The Story of Little Black
Sambo*, Chatto and Windus)

A Story Party at Green Hedges, which contained 'The Little Black Doll' (1949)

they reflected were those which were taken for granted by the majority of adults at that time'. This is not to excuse such racism or insensitivity, merely to place it in context – Bannerman and Blyton were writing against the backcloth of 'Empire' and 'white supremacy'. Much more despicable is the behaviour of publishers who – as in the case of Bannerman's *Little Black Sambo* – continue to publish such works, even in the multi-cultural societies of today.

The Three Golliwogs
(1968)

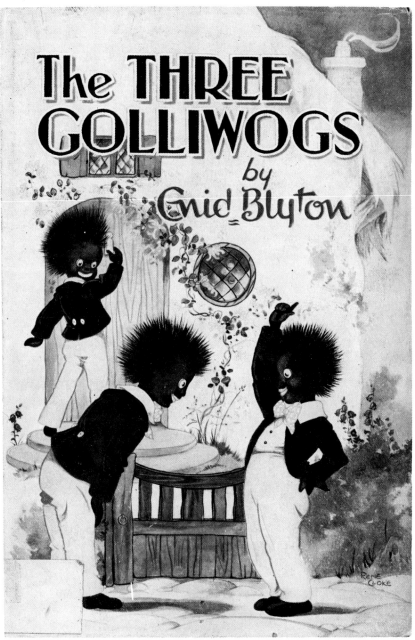

Golly, Woggie and Nigger
(1968)

'HERE COMES NODDY AGAIN'

The Noddy book which came in for so much criticism on the grounds of racism was the fourth in the series, *Here Comes Noddy Again*, published in 1951, in which we witness Noddy being mugged by three golliwogs.

NODDY

The term golliwog (derived from polliwog, a fifteenth-century description of a tadpole, with the emphasis given to black flesh) was first used in children's literature in 1895 by Florence K. Upton in her *The Adventures of Two Dutch Dolls and a 'Golliwogg'*. This story tells how two wooden dolls on the loose in a toyshop suddenly see a 'horrid sight' – the 'blackest gnome' (this is the 'golliwogg', an invention both in name and appearance of Upton's).

In *Here Comes Noddy Again* (1951) Noddy is busily earning his keep as a taxi-driver when one day a golliwog asks him if he will take him to a 'party in the Dark Wood at midnight'. Noddy is reluctant: 'There might be bad goblins about. It's so very very dark there.' However he agrees when the golliwog promises him a 'bag of sixpences'. At twelve o'clock Noddy gets out his little car but jumps when a voice came out of the darkness. 'Are you ready? I'm here!'

The Three Golliwogs
(1968)

> It was the golliwog. He was so black that Noddy couldn't see him, and bumped into him when he walked out to find him.
>
> 'Oh, sorry,' he said. 'Yes, I'm ready. Here is the car. Jump in.'
>
> The golliwog climbed in. Noddy switched on the lights of the little car. They weren't very good, only just enough to see by as he went down the streets of Toy-Town. The golliwog began to sing a peculiar song.
>
> > 'It isn't very good
> > In the Dark Dark Wood
> > In the middle of the night
> > When there isn't any light;
> > It isn't very good
> > In the Dark Dark Wood.'

Noddy asks the golliwog to be quiet, so the golliwog stops singing, but he keeps making 'chuckling noises' which Noddy doesn't appreciate: 'I wish I hadn't come,' he thinks. 'I do wish I hadn't come.'

On arrival Noddy asks where the party is: 'There isn't a party,' the golliwog says in a very nasty voice. 'This is a trap, Noddy. We want your car for ourselves. Get out at once!'

> Noddy couldn't move an inch. he was so full of alarm that he couldn't say a word. A trap! Whose trap? And why did they want his car?
>
> Then things happened very quickly. Three black

133

NODDY WRIGGLED AND SHOUTED AND WAILED

41

HERE COMES NODDY AGAIN!

Then the driver leaned out and told the others to get him Noddy's dear little trousers and shoes.

Soon Noddy had no clothes on at all. He wriggled and shouted and wailed. "No, no, no! I want my hat, I want my shirt. You bad, wicked golliwogs! How dare you steal my things?"

But it wasn't a bit of good. What could the little nodding man do against four big strong golliwogs? Nothing at all.

The golliwogs piled into the little red and yellow car. Two were in front, two sat in the back of the car. One of them had Noddy's hat

42

faces suddenly appeared in the light of the car's lamps, and three golliwogs came running to the car. In a trice they had hold of poor Noddy and pulled him right out of his little car.

The muggers leave Noddy 'naked' and crying: 'I'm little Noddy and I'm all alone and lost!' With the help of a mouse he finds Big-Ears' toadstool house, and in due course Big-Ears and a Toy-Town policeman capture the golliwogs (in a sack) and return Noddy's car and clothes to him. 'So the policeman drove off with the sack of squealing, squirming golliwogs, and Big-Ears followed on his little bicycle, ringing the bell madly.'

To the publishers' credit a new version of the series has been produced, and in keeping with some overseas countries – France, for example, which buys enormous quantities of *Oui Oui* (Noddy's French name) – the golliwogs have been phased out

'Noddy wriggled ...'
(1951, *Here Comes Noddy Again*)

'How dare you steal my things?'
(1951, *Here Comes Noddy Again*)

and replaced (in the case of Britain) by goblins and bears. In the 1986 version the text has also, of necessity, been changed. We no longer have 'three black faces suddenly appeared in the light', rather 'three goblins jumped out from behind a tree'. In addition he is not left naked, merely shoeless and hatless! We no longer have a sack full of 'squealing, squirming golliwogs', now, it's a simple case of a 'sack of goblins'.

Interestingly enough in the case of Britain, the old series (which is still issued) and the new golliwog-free series match each other in terms of sales, almost certainly because Van der Beek's drawings are superior. In addition, the adult parent buying the books for his or her child would recognise only the old editions.

Enid Blyton's reaction to criticisms of the Noddy books was that she had written far more *good* golliwogs into her stories than bad. She claimed somewhat naively, that:

> Golliwogs are merely lovable black toys, not Negroes. Teddy bears are also toys, but if there happens to be a naughty one in my books for younger children, this does not mean that I hate bears!

'Plop! Plop!'
(1951, *Here Comes Noddy Again*)

To Ban or Not to Ban?

Many people talk of the alleged 'banning' of Blyton books by librarians, but as Jeremy Lewis (1982) amusingly puts it, 'like wife-swapping in the Home Counties, the banning of Blyton seems to have been more a matter of rumour than of fact'. Certainly there are well-documented cases, as in Nottingham in 1964 onwards, when libraries phased out the buying of Blyton books, but the matter is clearly more complex and less simple than it appears at first sight. To begin with, the reported 'phasing out' or purchase in 'limited quantities' was by no means a general policy.

Sheila Ray (1982) is probably closest to the truth when she argues that the first public manifestations of the 'Blyton problem' were in the early 1950s when there was increased concern about her excessive popularity and 'escapism'. She was considered too 'light-weight', as well as possibly racist. As there was more money to spend on children's books in the 1950s – and children could *buy* the books themselves from all manner of outlets – some librarians considered that the monies should be spent on the 'best in children's literature', and thus books by Blyton, Johns (creator of 'Biggles') and Richmal Crompton (creator of 'William') were not replaced as they wore out. Sheila Ray also suggests that it could well have been that libraries were not necessarily anti-Blyton, but that her enormous output made it necessary to be

shoes as well!" shouted Mr Plod.
"Hurry back, and bring a big cake, Big-Ears. I feel well again and I'm going to have a party to celebrate!"
And that's just what they did. Mr Plod brought the goblins along to say they were sorry. Big-Ears made them polish the

(1986 edition, *Here Comes Noddy Again*, Purnell)

selective. Of course another explanation, much simpler, is that some librarians exercised their rights of choice and were merely guilty of snobbishness or elitism.

NODDY AND HIS CRITICS

Like the majority of the Blyton creations – the adventure stories, fantasy stories, girls' school stories – Noddy continues to be bought and 'read by' the intended audience. Critics, however, as we saw earlier with Colin Welch's *Encounter* piece, have enjoyed themselves at Noddy's expense. In a sense it has been a back-handed compliment: indeed a sign of his importance.

In 1961 David Holbrook argued that in Noddy books nothing was rendered 'mysterious, discomforting or troublesome', as in 'Toyland every difficulty may be overcome by some such device as a jolly magic rubber, and everything is tractable', while in 1977 Richard Hoggart condemned Noddy for 'perpetuating stereotypes of class'. Margery Fisher in her *Who's Who in Children's Books* (1975) describes him as a 'monotonously infantile character' – which is rather unfair to children – who is:

> frequently heard to say that he doesn't like being sensible but would far rather be silly, (and who) seems to have been put together from the weakest and least desirable attributes of childhood. It is hard to explain the persistent popularity of these trivial, repetitive stories with their small, retarded, masochistic hero.

Edward Blishen, in his pugnacious article 'Who's afraid of Enid Blyton?' (1977), argues that the essence of the Noddy stories is

NODDY

that a reader's imagination is not roused, rather it is 'positively damped'. He complains of the language – 'lovely', 'nice', 'dear', 'little, 'cosy', 'peculiar', 'horrid', 'very' – which, for him, is not the language of the child, but rather 'the language used when talking to children by ill-informed aunts who suppose children must be wrapped in verbal wool'. Blishen describes Noddy as:

> a wooden toy whose only positive characteristic is the uncomfortable one that his head, attached to his body by a spring, can be set nodding by anyone who cares to give it a tap...[and that]...the heights of euphoria are achieved when Noddy exclaims 'Aren't people nice?', though clearly, when he is excited into this observation, he has forgotten the Giggle Goblins and all those 'horrid' characters who aren't to be made 'nice' even by a 'good spanking'.

ANOTHER JOB FOR NODDY
The garage had a toy petrol station, and was really rather grand. Tiny cars drove up for petrol. Others came in for cleaning and polishing.

The owner of the garage was a golliwog with a very black, smiling face. He looked at the little nodding man and liked him.
"Yes, you can come and clean cars for me," he said. "My man is away. You can have his job till he comes back."

(1950, *Hurrah for Little Noddy*, Sampson Low)

Blishen concludes that the popularity of the books is due to Blyton's undemanding writing, her use of a small vocabulary and a small set of basic narrative elements, and finally, that 'her voice bumbles in the ear like that of some universal mum, a lowest common denominator of mummishness, alternately cosy and cross'.

And of course there have been, as we have already noted, justifiable criticisms of racism, and also critics who have detected 'murky undertones' in Noddy's relationship with Big-Ears:

> 'If you can squeeze into my tiny bed, you can sleep with me tonight,' said Big-Ears ... They squashed into Big-Ears' tiny, soft bed, put their arms round one another to stop themselves from rolling out, and fell fast asleep. (*Hurrah for Little Noddy*, 1950)

So why then is Noddy so popular? Nicholas Tucker (1981) offers a number of reasons, while at the same time unfavourably comparing him to A.A. Milne's 'Pooh' stories. First, Noddy *tends* to live a relatively trouble-free life as an innocent in a safe environment, Toyland: this, Tucker argues, allows the younger child to relax and enjoy the book. Secondly, although the fact that Noddy is similar to but more 'naive and stupid' than 'real children' may appeal to readers, making them feel superior, he also receives 'far more praise than blame from other characters', and indeed it is not at all unusual for a story to end with a 'virtual paean' in favour of the little nodding man. To this sort of praise, Noddy will often respond with one of his impromptu songs, again to

(1986, *Hurrah for Little Noddy*, Purnell)

The next morning Noddy decided to explore Toyland again. As he passed the garage, its owner, Bobby Bear, called out to him in a friendly voice:

"Hello there Noddy! We're in need of some extra help today. Would you like to come and give us a hand?"

Noddy loved cars. In the garage there were cars of every colour: red, blue, yellow, green and orange. When Bobby Bear asked him if he would polish them Noddy was pleased.

Noddy worked very hard and soon he could see his face in the shine on the bonnet of every car.

"If only I had a car of my own!" sighed Noddy.

"You're a good worker Noddy!" smiled Bobby Bear. "I'm very pleased with your work – here's your pay packet."

general admiration, and then 'motor away to his own diminutive, cosy house'. Tucker adds that this other, more independent and competent side to Noddy can in turn 'act as fuel for children's lingering fantasies about the possibility of a similar type of existence for themselves, even though they may continue to laugh at him in other ways'.

This of course is another way of expressing the opinion that, quite simply, the creation of Noddy is yet another example of Enid Blyton's ability to understand the dreams of the child and to write stories through the child's eyes. As Sheila Ray (1982) observes:

> Noddy has something in common with the heroes and heroines of many modern stories for young children; like Paddington, Pooh, Babar and Pippa Longstocking,

he combines the innocence and naivety of the child with some of the advantages of being an adult. Noddy's main advantage is that he owns and drives a car, but he also lives on his own and exercises a certain amount of independence.

Noddy and Big-Ears
(1984, *Noddy Treasury*, Purnell)

One of the important lessons to be drawn from the Noddy books is that of Enid Blyton's 'ability' to write at all levels, for all sorts of age groups. Although highly successful at writing for eight- to twelve-year-old children, she demonstrates a general ability with the Noddy books. Indeed she *deliberately* wrote in the language of every age-group, for children from 'five to fifteen', so that those who discovered her works when very young would remain faithful for the next decade.

Like him or loathe him, Noddy himself has a place in the hall of fame with colleagues such as Mickey Mouse (1928-) based on Disney himself, Paddington Bear (1958-) the marmalade-eater from 'darkest Peru', and Rupert (1920-) the check-trousered inhabitant of Nutwood. Meanwhile, Noddy continues to outlive his creator...

CHAPTER
— 6 —

THE BLYTON SECRET

In the 1950s Enid Blyton had clearly been upset by the actions of those librarians who had ceased to stock her books – although this action did not in any way affect her sales – but she was far more distressed by the persistent rumours that she was not responsible for the writing of all her stories. Some cynics argued that Enid ran a 'company of ghost writers' for it was hard to believe that one woman could produce such quantities of work on her own. Not surprisingly; in 1949 she produced thirty-three books, with thirty-one the year after, while in 1951 there are at least thirty-seven titles to her name, although in 1952 she wrote a 'mere' thirty-five. (It is possible that these figures could be slight underestimates, as there could be more Blyton work around as yet unaccounted for.)

In 1955 she tried to discredit the rumours through legal action against those involved and was partly successful in doing so. At the time she wrote an interesting letter to her solicitor on the matter.

> This is very damaging, not only to my books, but to me. I am such a public figure now, and well trusted, as you know, and run many clubs and societies which bring in money, that I absolutely *must* have these rumours cleared up – for who is going to believe I am honest if I don't even write my own books!...In the last month or two we have had rumours from Australia that I am dead and someone else is writing my books. Rumours from S Africa that I am dead and no longer write my books and rumours, also from S Africa, that I am alive, but do not write my books and now here is a librarian with the same slander...

'I expect so,' said Peter. 'Oh, Jean — do let's go and speak to them all! I'm sure they won't be frightened.'

„Ich glaube ja", antwortete Klaus. Dann sagte er: „Komm, Marlies, wir gehen hin und reden mit ihnen. Ich bin mir ganz sicher, daß sie keine Angst haben werden."

Enid was indeed alive, but both her and Kenneth's health was slowly deteriorating. Enid herself was now a woman of almost sixty years of age, and presumably would have preferred such rumours, and the anxiety they caused, to cease.

As Barbara Stoney (1974) notes, Green Hedges 'continued to run smoothly and efficiently with its regular cook, housemaid, gardener and chauffeur, and Enid's well-invested income alone ... was more than sufficient to keep up their present standard of living for the rest of their lives, without her writing another word.' They regularly entertained at home, ran a Rolls-Royce, a Bentley and a small sports car and lunched weekly at the Savoy with business associates. However, during a round of golf together in May 1957, Enid suddenly complained of 'feeling faint' and 'breathless'. Kenneth took her home and called for a heart specialist friend from London. Barbara Stoney adds that

> When he arrived Enid was showing some agitation, for Kenneth's quick action in summoning the cardiologist

The Bonfire Folk (1985 edition, *The Bonfire Folk*, Award Press)

The German bonfire folk (1986 edition, *Wolle Ihr Mal die Zwerge Sehan?*)

Enid and Darrell
(Source: Darrell Waters
Group)

had convinced her that she was seriously ill and memories of her father's fatal heart attack all those years before, which she had tried so hard to bury, resurfaced. She was sure that she had a condition similar to his and felt that the 'attack' was by way of a warning to her that she had, as Kenneth had often told her, been working too hard.

The cardiologist however diagnosed that her discomfort and pain were due not to a diseased heart, but to a 'digestive malfunction, brought on, he thought, by Enid's many long hours hunched over her typewriter'. Enid would not believe this, and Kenneth, for 'reasons known only to himself, appears to have encouraged this self-deception'. Indeed when Enid's daughters, Gillian and Imogen, returned home from university at the end of the term, Kenneth informed them that their mother had suffered a 'heart attack' and had been told to rest. As to the question of why Kenneth should have kept up such a pretence with Enid's daughters as well as herself, Stoney suggests that the most feasible explanation seems to be that 'he had already noticed certain signs in her behaviour which indicated a breakdown in her health in other directions, and sought to delay this in some way by curtailing her activities, without divulging his own fears as to the real nature of the illness'.

However this enforced rest from work did not particularly alleviate the difficulties, rather it 'brought about other, more distressing, side-effects'. Barbara Stoney reports that Enid confided to her daughter Imogen that, 'whereas previously she had always been able to ride disaster by "keeping busy" she was now finding her thoughts "closing in" upon her'.

> It is easy to suppose that, now she was no longer directing most of her thoughts towards the fantasy worlds of her own creation, some of the harsh realities she had for so long 'put away' were at last rising to the surface – aided, perhaps, by the sedative drug she had been prescribed. So much of her life she had kept hidden from those around her, and what little she had revealed had been embroidered into stories she now half-believed herself. Perhaps with time now to brood over some of the unhappy events of the past, triggered off no doubt by the reminder of her father's sudden death, she may even have experienced certain feelings of guilt over her treatment of those once close to her.

"You are not to talk to us like that," said the biggest doll, called Angelina. "We don't like those mice. We shall chase them out of the playroom every time they come."

So, whenever the real little mice popped their heads out of their hole, the big dolls ran at them, and chased them back. Angelina banged the mother-mouse on the nose with a spoon, and the mother-mouse squealed with pain.

"How unkind you are!" said the clockwork mouse, angrily. "You know they are my friends.

The Spanish clockwork mouse
(1986, *El Raton Mecanico En Apules*)

The Clockwork Mouse in Trouble
(*The Clockwork Mouse in Trouble*, Collins)

«No debes hablarnos así —dijo la muñeca más grande, que se llamaba Angelina—. A nosotras esos ratones no nos gustan. Les echaremos del cuarto de jugar siempre que vengan a él.»

Así lo hicieron; apenas los verdaderos ratones asomaban la cabeza, las grandes muñecas se les echaban encima y les obligaban a meterse de nuevo en su agujero. Angelina golpeó en el hocico a la madre de los ratones con una cuchara, y la madre gimió de dolor.

«¡Qué poco amable eres! —dijo el ratón mecánico enojado—. Sabes que son amigos

Hugh had long given up attempts to visit his daughters, or indeed to contest the issue any further, but Enid 'must have known in her heart that she had not treated him fairly by going back on her original promise to him'. It was also too late to be reconciled with her mother, who had died seven years earlier following an illness lasting a number of years. Enid had not seen her mother for thirty years, despite 'her mother's pleadings – particularly during her latter years – to see the daughter from whom she had

143

so long been estranged'. Enid's reply had always been that she
was 'too busy', the reason she gave to others for not attending her
mother's funeral. Enid's own daughters knew nothing of their
grandmother until after her death, and neither of Enid's hus-
bands were ever given an explanation as to why they were never
allowed to meet their mother-in-law. 'They had no reason to
disbelieve Enid's story, also told to her daughters, that she had
been "brought up" by the Attenboroughs, having run away from
home as a "young girl".' Stoney observes that when Enid was
busy with her work she could shut out 'any thoughts which
conflicted with that of her popular image, but now that she was
forced into an unhappy introspection of herself perhaps she did
not like what she saw. She found it increasingly difficult to sleep
and became even more depressed and irritable.'

The years went by and Enid had to accept that her powers were
diminishing, and at the same time that Kenneth himself was no
longer a healthy man. In early 1967, during a 'rare journey into
reality' Enid telephoned a surprised Hanly Blyton, who had not
heard from his sister for nearly seventeen years, and begged him
to visit her. Stoney unhappily reports that Kenneth had been
taken into hospital for a short period, her daughters were both
away from home and she was, she told him, 'desperately lonely'.

> Realising, with some concern, that Enid was obviously
> a sick woman, he made the journey from Kent a few
> days later, only to find his sister quite unable to recall
> her urgent summons and barely able to recognise him.
> Once the realisation came that this 'strange man' was
> indeed her brother, she was obsessed with the thought
> that she must immediately return 'home' with him to
> Beckenham and 'Mother and Father' and this idea
> persisted long after he had left. She could remember
> only the happy times the little family had spent to-
> gether before their father had left them, and all the pain
> of parting had mercifully been obliterated.

In late 1967 Kenneth died, and after a brief period when she
returned to normal, Enid relapsed into her 'old dream world and
the desire to return to her childhood home once more obsessed
her'. In the months that followed Enid declined both physically
and mentally, and some three months after being admitted to a
Hampstead nursing home, she died peacefully in her sleep on 28
November 1968.

Enid died in a year that saw some of the most violent changes
in recent history – the assassinations of Robert Kennedy and the
Reverend Martin Luther King; student riots; Soviet troops occu-

pied Czechoslovakia; crimes of violence in the USA had doubled since 1960 – and it was a year also that saw the deaths of other writers like Upton Sinclair and John Steinbeck, and the publication of John Updike's *Couples*, Gore Vidal's *Myra Breckinridge* and Arthur Hailey's *Airport*. It was also the year that Joe Orton's *Loot* was first staged. All of this was a far cry from the world of Enid Blyton.

What were *her* methods, and where does she stand as a figure in children's literature?

Enid in 1959 operating a Noddy puppet (The Photo Source)

ENID BLYTON AND CHILDREN'S LITERATURE

Enid could type out 10,000 words of finished copy at one sitting: how? In her autobiography, *The Story of My Life* (1952) she tells her readers that:

> If I sit in my chair and shut my eyes for a minute or two, in comes the story I am waiting for, all ready and complete in my imagination.
>
> I sit in my chair and think, 'Now today I am going to begin a new book. What shall it be? Adventure? Circus? Nature? Fairy-tale? Mystery? I think it is time for a fairy-tale! A fairy tale it shall be!'
>
> I have to find two things when I write a book. I have to find my characters, of course, and the setting for the story – the place where everything happens. So I shut my eyes, and I look into my mind's eye. You know what that is, don't you? We all have one.

Enid adds that she 'could write a whole book at one sitting if only I didn't have to eat or sleep,' that she could type 'ten or twelve thousand words a day', and that she could indeed 'write much more if only my arms didn't get tired of being poised over my typewriter'. Finally, in a mini-lecture on the psychology of the mind, she adds that after quickly writing 60,000 words she would not be tired as she would have used her 'imagination' as distinct from her 'brain'. Brain work *is* tiring. 'Using one's imagination is not.'

Peter McKeller (1977, orig. 1957), who has attempted to study Enid Blyton's methods, reports that Enid herself used the image of a 'private cinema screen': 'I shut my eyes for a few minutes, with my portable typewriter on my knee; I make my mind a blank and wait – and then, as clearly as I would see real children, my characters stand before me in my mind's eye...the story is

Gordon Gardner (L) as Julian of the 'Five' and Bunny May (R) in *Noddy in Toyland* (The Photo Source)

enacted almost as if I had a private cinema screen there.' Enid adds that she does not know 'what anyone is going to say or do', or what is 'going to happen', and moreover she is in the 'happy position of being able to write a story and read it for the first time, at one and the same time'. McKellar quotes one of Enid's observations:

'Sometimes,' she writes, 'a character makes a joke, a really funny one that makes me laugh as I type it on my paper, and I think: "Well, I couldn't have thought of that myself in a hundred years!" And then I think: "Well, who *did* think of it?" '

Incidentally, Joyce Grenfell, in a sketch from her 'Joyce Grenfell Requests the Pleasure' series (1954), amusingly sends up Enid's 'methods'.

Hullo, boys and girls. I was so pleased when you asked me to come along and tell you how I write my books for children. Well, of course, the answer is – I don't. No, my books write themselves for me...
Well as you know, children, I write lots and lots of books for you and this is how I set about it. First of all I go upstairs to my Hidey Hole – well, this is really just a

great big upstairs workroom but I like to call it my Hidey Hole. I pin a notice on the door and it says: 'Gone to Make Believe Land.' This is just my way of saying: 'Please don't come and bother me because a book is writing itself for me and we mustn't disturb it, must we?'

Then I put a clean white sheet of paper in my typewriter and I sit down in front of it and I close my eyes. And what do I see? I see a rambling old house in Cornwall. And I hear seagulls – and I see children – one – two – *three* children scrambling up the cliffs because they are very nearly late for tea, and their names are Jennifer-Ann, and Robin-John, and the little one is called Midge – because he is the littlest one. (Oh yes, he has a proper name. It's Anthony Timothy Jeremy Michael and he doesn't like porridge – but, we won't tell anyone, will we?)

Joking apart, her method seems both extraordinary and unique, if her own account is correct. There is very little to add, except that although her method led to numerous mistakes, repetitiveness and a somewhat limited vocabulary, it was none the less highly successful. And besides it was, for her, the only way she could write.

We have already noted how Enid Blyton's work was widely

'Great news darling — I'm signed up to star wit h Noddy in "Noddy and Big Ears" at Buck House'

Prince Charles and children's literature
(*Daily Mail*, 7 September 1984)

criticised over the years, and indeed by the mid-1970s it was 'generally accepted' that she was a 'bad writer; her attitudes were suspect, her characterization thought to be shallow and stereotyped, her plots unrealistic, her vocabulary repetitive and undemanding'. Sheila Ray concludes (1982) that she 'had come to be regarded as a touchstone for what is bad in writing for children'. Edward Blishen meanwhile, a little earlier in 1967, was 'saddened' by the number of readers who praised her work as a 'useful step in the fostering of reading ability', and his 'gloom' was not lightened by the 'assertion of one of them that reading Miss Blyton's adventure stories is an effective bridge to Buchan, Stevenson and Dumas. From the Famous Five to the Three Musketeers in one step?' Margery Fisher, on the other hand, in reviewing Enid Blyton's *The Mystery of the Strange Bundle* (1973), said she was 'sorry to see that a new generation is to be encouraged to feed' on what she 'honestly believed' to be 'slow poison'.

Sheila Ray (1982) reserves her 'strongest criticism' of Enid Blyton for her vocabulary: 'she makes use of a very limited number of words and seems at times to have an almost pathological fear of using a word which might not be understood by all her readers.' One might retort, so what? Shouldn't we use words which our readers are able to understand? In any case this is one area where the critics may have overstated the case, for as Nicholas Tucker (1981) observes, in the last ten pages of *The Mystery of the Spiteful Letters* (1946) one can find 'righteous', 'mystification', 'reprimanded', 'courteous', 'anonymous' and 'deduction' – hardly an 'over-adventurous vocabulary, but certainly not the baby-talk that critics have sometimes suggested'.

Fred Inglis, in *The Promise of Happiness* (1981), subtitled 'Value and Meaning in Children's Fiction' tells of how he himself read Blyton as a child – 'the Malory Towers stories, the Sea, Valley, Island of Adventure, the endless Five series', – and that he 'certainly took in from these books their overpowering snobbery, the meanness and vengefulness of so much of the morality, the herd victimization of silliness and vanity'. He read the books for their 'utter unreality' and the 'untaxing safety of their stereotypes', and adds that 'reading Enid Blyton is much like reading comics. Awful, and indeed worse than comics, because so lacking in their lurid high spirits and loud vulgarity. Awful, but unimportant.' Inglis concludes that children read Blyton in order to avoid 'using their imaginations'. On this point Inglis is simply wrong. Wallace Hildick (1970), for example, is far more perceptive when, in trying to understand the *universal* popularity of Enid Blyton, he comments that:

A child of limited intelligence, who has nevertheless

148

learned to read with reasonable fluency will derive great pleasure from a Blyton book's mechanical easiness alone; while a child of higher intelligence – to whom that form of easiness is irrelevant – will derive great pleasure from using it as an efficient screen on which to project fantasies of his own. (And for the former type of child there is then the psychological bonus of being able to read and enjoy a book which a more gifted schoolfriend also obviously enjoys).

Finally there are the criticisms of Aiden Chambers who, writing in 1973, complained of Blyton's 'triviality, linguistically impoverished style, anaemia in plot and characterization, and clichéd, stereotyped ideas', while writing later in 1985 he argues that Blyton 'so allies herself with her desired readers that she fails them because she never takes them further than they are':

> She is a female Peter Pan, the kind of suffocating adult who prefers children never to grow up, because then she can enjoy their pretty foibles and dominate them by her adult superiority. This betrayal of childhood seeps through her stories; we see it as the underlying characteristic of her children who all really want to dominate each other as well as the adults.

Richard Hoggart put the same point another way when he argued that the 'strongest objection to the more trivial entertainments is not that they prevent their readers from becoming highbrow, but that they make it harder for people without an intellectual bent to become wise in their own way.' This is the crux of the issue: the question of whether or not Enid Blyton's work has much value is actually a question about the purpose and meaning of children's literature – should children get what they want?

BLYTON'S 'NOT SO HIDDEN' GENIUS

We have quite rightly documented the criticisms that have been made against Enid Blyton's work, but what of her positive virtues, other than the fact that she clearly gives children what they want?

Nicholas Tucker (1977) suggests, for example, that her adventure books, to cite just one example, were more successful than often considered.

> Her plots forge ahead almost in an ecstasy of action. It
> is untrue to imagine they were always easily predic-
> table; the excitement and happy ending may have
> been, but not the details in between, and to that extent
> she can keep even the most sceptical adult reader
> uncertain until the last few pages.

While Donald Fry (1985), almost apologetically, comments that
'children learn to read by reading', and that therefore the 'only
way to facilitate their learning to read is to make reading easy for
them' – 'and that is what Enid Blyton manages to do'. Sheila Ray
(1982) makes the same point about Blyton's work as a 'gateway'
to further reading when she argues that there is a 'general feeling
that the kind of books which Enid Blyton wrote are needed to
help children achieve fluency in reading, and that no other
author has been able to meet this need so effectively'. Nicholas
Tucker (1981) simply states that her achievement was 'to offer
children long stories they could actually read and understand for
themselves'.

Although there is no agreement about the way in which
children's books should be judged, the acrimonious debate
surrounding Enid Blyton's work does raise the question as to
why she was *so* unpopular with the majority of adult critics, and
'phased out' by some librarians. Indeed as Nicholas Tucker (1981)
argues, one cannot say that 'all adult criticism of Enid Blyton is
based on fear and envy; yet some extra explanation seems
needed to account for the degree of hostility she has always
provoked.' Other writers have produced books using a meagre
vocabulary, little characterisation, predictability in plot, and
reactionary attitudes, but none have suffered the critics' and
adults' sword to the degree that Blyton has – not even the likes of
W.E. Johns, Richmal Crompton and Frank Richards. The reason
for the excessive and somewhat unwarranted criticism is actually
two-fold: Enid Blyton simply wrote too much and was too popular for many to accept – 'the building up and knocking down of
heroes' – and she aligned herself too closely to the children for
whom she wrote.

For example, the disdain shown for Blyton by Frank Whitehead *et al.*'s (1977) School's Council Research study *Children and
Their Books* when faced with the evidence of Blyton's overwhelm-
ing popularity is odious. Simply another case of adults' believing
that they both know what is 'good' for children and that they
have the almost omnipotent right to choose for their children.
Indeed Gillian Avery (1975) suggests that children's reading
seems to fall into three categories: the books adults promote,
those that they merely tolerate and 'trash' that they would like to
withold altogether.

C.S. Lewis, the deservedly respected creator of the *Narnia* books, in a well-known article 'On Three Ways of Writing for Children' (1952), is more subtly but equally censorious. He argues that there are 'three ways in which those who write for children may approach their work', two 'good ways and one that is generally a bad way'. One 'good way' is to produce a printed

(*Enid Blyton's Magazine*, 1959)

story from an oral one read to a 'real' child, and in this method there is 'no question of "children" conceived as a strange species whose habits you have "made up" '. The 'bad way' is to consider 'writing for children as a special department of "giving the public what it wants" ', while the third way, which is the only one he would ever have considered using himself, consists in

> writing a children's story because a children's story is the best art-form for something you have to say: just as a composer might write a Dead March not because there was a public funeral in view but because certain musical ideas that had occurred to him went best into that form.

The implication being that when the children's story is 'simply the right form for what the author has to say, then of course readers who want to hear that will read or re-read it at any age'. Lewis went further: 'I am almost inclined to set up as a canon that a children's story which is enjoyed only by children, is a bad children's story' and, put another way, that 'the only imaginative works we ought to grow out of are those which it would have been better not to have read at all.'

Using this criterion, of course, Enid Blyton's works would be not worth reading, as she is seen as someone who 'writes down' to children at worst or sees the world solely through children's eyes, at best. However C.S. Lewis's position is one of sheer arrogance, and almost imperialistic in its implications. As Robert Leeson (1985) rightly points out, Lewis's point of view 'marks a trend in criticism moving on from establishing "adult" standards, to the elimination of the child from the evaluation of the literature'.

Actually the story of Enid Blyton is indeed partly a story of attempted censorship of her books by those who have felt disinclined towards her work. The censorship issue is as riddled with hypocrisy as is the case of excessive criticism arising out of the envy of her popularity. As Nicholas Tucker (1981) expresses it, whenever 'adults have the freedom to choose their own reading, they often themselves are attracted by rather different, less high-minded writing than they may wish their children to read'. Tucker importantly adds that it is in fact unrealistic to expect children's literature

> always to avoid any reflection of its audience's immaturity, even when such reflections may sometimes seem crude and perhaps unfeeling. If all children's authors consistently write above the heads of their

audience, and if the institutions which provide books for the young become over-fastidious in their selections, rather than children themselves changing, children's literature itself could become increasingly remote from those for whom it is supposed to be catering.

In any case even if we desired censorship (of *any* children's reading) it would be a 'quite hopeless' task, for as Anthony Storr (1980) argues, if the 'normal child were as susceptible to the effects of literature as parents sometimes fear, we should have to proscribe reading altogether'. He adds: 'A man told me that his masochistic interest in male slavery had been stimulated in childhood by pictures of the building of the Pyramids. Are we to ban history books on this account?' In any event censorship of children's literature appears to go against a solid cyclical historial pattern in British children's books. Frank Eyre in *British Children's Books in the Twentieth Century* (1971, orig. 1952) explains:

> It is possible to discern a cyclical pattern in British children's books throughout the centuries, consisting of a continual alternation between the most determinedly moral stories calculated to improve and uplift young readers, and books designed to be read for enjoyment. The former kind of book appears to reign supreme for about half a century, but towards the end a violent reaction begins.

Eyre expands and argues that:

> This alternation between 'what children like' and 'what children ought to have' can be traced throughout the brief history of children's publishing in Britain and is closely related to parallel changes in social thought and behaviour. Thus the Puritan reaction against the alleged licentiousness of the way of life they sought to suppress was paralleled by the introduction of a host of 'goodly' books designed to replace the romances, the *Gesta Romanorum*, the Bestiaries, and the like, which up to that time had been the principal source of reading for children...

and moreover that:

> With each swing of the pendulum, however, the reaction towards didacticism became less pronounced and the books produced became easier to read and enjoy. It

'Realism' in children's literature (*Sunday People*, 21 September 1986)

is possible, therefore, to see the whole history of British children's publishing as a development towards freedom – freedom of expression, thought, and, above all, of imagination. The idea that a children's book of whatever type ought to have a 'purpose' had by the end of the nineteenth century been overthrown.

Eyre concludes that the movement 'towards undiluted enjoyment in children's books gradually gained momentum, and if the previous history had been one of struggle for freedom the history of the present century has been one almost of licence'.

A CONUNDRUM

We began this book with a remark of Philip Thody's, who regarded Enid Blyton as 'depressingly normal'. This Enid certainly wasn't. The sheer output of her work, for example, made sure of that. And clearly psychologically she was a most complex personality: it can be reasonably assumed that the early 'loss' of her father gave her both the energy to write her books and imposed a shape on some of them. In particular, her school stories bear the imprint of someone disenchanted with her mother. And George, the heroine of her 'Famous Five' series, was firmly rooted in her own personality.

Her books do tend towards repetitiveness, but as we have seen, the talk of her meagre vocabulary is somewhat exaggerated, as is the claim that she *never* developed characters or plots. As for Noddy, he was simply a stroke of immense ingenuity. And on top of all this, Enid Blyton had a pragmatism and a business-like acumen second to none in the world of writing.

Through her work she staunchly defended the rights of children to have books written for them both reflecting the way the world is and also a world they would desire. She captured the child's daydreams and fantasies.

As for the lack of 'realism', which undoubtedly existed, presumably we wish for books of all hues. We should, for example, welcome the contribution of Judy Blume who, in a number of novels, like *Blubber* (1974) a story of a fat girl, *Deenie* (1973), whose heroine suffers from a curvature of the spine, and *Are you there, God? It's me, Margaret* (1970), where an eleven-year-old girl hopes for the onset of puberty and expresses hope in the form of prayers – 'I just told my mother I wanted a bra. Please help me grow, God. You know where' – has brought the 'teenage novel' to a new stage of realism.

> I rang Val's bell. She let me in. I got there in time to meet her mother's boyfriend, Seymour Chandler. He doesn't really look anything like a boyfriend. He looks more like a grandfather to me. His hair is silver and he's kind of fat. But Mrs Lewis looked beautiful. I wouldn't want to have a mother that's good looking. I'd spend all my time worrying about how I was going to turn out compared to her. Not that Val is ugly. She's okay. But she doesn't look like her mother.
>
> Val introduced me to Mr Chandler. She said, 'Seymour, this is my friend Karen. Her father lives upstairs. He's getting a divorce.' Then Val told me, 'Seymour's divorced too.'
>
> 'That's right,' Seymour said. 'I am. Twice, as a matter of fact.' Then he laughed. (Judy Blume, 1979, *It's Not The End of The World*)

Similarly we should welcome the sophisticated books of writers like Nina Bawden, in her 'realistic' *The Peppermint Pig* (1975), Susan Cooper and Penelope Lively and books like E.B. White's (1952) marvellous *Charlotte's Web*, where Wilbur, the pig, is saved from his bacon destiny by Charlotte, a spider, who brings about what seems to be a series of miracles to keep Wilbur from the butcher's knife. There should be room too for Enid Blyton

Edward Blishen (1977) puts the case for a diverse offering very well:

> The world of children's fiction is constantly under attack: for the pure quantity of it, for its over-lofty quality, for its mediocrity. I don't want to seem complacent – but imagine if it were under attack for its paucity, its absence of fineness and daring, its lack of journeyman work and of the sort of unpretentious material that may be an important ingredient in the nourishment of any reader whatever. We need, I think, to be grateful that the literary offering we can make to the young is so diverse and presents them with the fullest opportunity of arriving at notions of their own about the best, the good, the indifferent and the bad.

In a highly perceptive evaluation of Enid Blyton, Robert Leeson (1985) argues that 'Blyton was a communicator', she 'wrote direct to the kids', she 'answered their letters by the thousand', she 'encouraged children to write to each other, town to country and so on'. Leeson suggests that 'anyone who thinks "easy" writing is easy writing, that it means less effort, should study her life and find some of the reasons why there are not many like her.' He concludes that:

> She absorbed the world of children and gave it back to them. Her first writings were directly for the children she taught. As someone said of her, 'she knew just how children like a story to be.' That was the ace in her pack. She started them young: no complaints about the customer from her. She fed the children, from four to fourteen, on themselves. She satisfied them and left them hungry for more of the same.

This would be the kind of tribute that Enid herself might have appreciated. She does not emerge as an heroic figure, or even a likeable one, but a writer she definitely was.

INDEX

INDEX

159